# WARRIORS

0-8054-6262-7
Dewey Decimal Classification: 248.832
Subject Heading: YOUNG MEN — RELIGIOUS LIFE
Library of Congress Card Catalog Number: 95-11875

Unless otherwise noted, Scripture is taken from the New American Standard Bible, © the Lockman Foundation, 1960, 1962, 1963, 1968, 1971, 1972, 1973, 1975, 1977, used by permission. Other passages are marked AMP, The Amplified Bible, Old Testament ©1962, 1974 by Zondervan Publishing House, used by permission, and the New Testament ©The Lockman Foundation 1954, 1958, 1987, used by permission; and TLB, The Living Bible, ©Tyndale House Publishers, Wheaton, Ill., 1971, used by permission.

**Library of Congress Cataloging-in-Publication Data**

Sirotnak, Tom. 1958–
    Warriors / by Tom Sirotnak with Ken Walker.

    p.  cm.
Includes bibliographical references.

ISBN 0-8054-6262-7
    1. Spiritual warfare.  2. Young men—Religious life.  3. Young men—conduct of life.  I. Walker, Ken, 1957–.   II. Title
    BV4509.5.S4729    1995

    248.8'42—dc20                     95-11875

# WARRIORS

## Tom Sirotnak
## with Kenneth Walker

Broadman & Holman Publishers
Nashville, Tennessee

# HAVE YOU HEARD WHAT PEOPLE ARE SAYING ABOUT WARRIORS?

*Warriors* is a book that bridges the gap between a disillusioned, uninterested young generation and the call of destiny. This book checks deep within the heart of a young man and unashamedly forces him to answer this question, "Am I fulfilling my destiny or just wasting my time?"

—*A. C. Green*

This generation doesn't belong to the devil; it belongs to Jesus. In *Warriors* Tom Sirotnak captures the heartbeat of a confused, apathetic, self-seeking generation. *Warriors* is a battle plan to achieve your destiny and impact this world for the glory of God. This book is an essential foundation builder for every young disciple of Christ.

So many in life passively wait for their ship to come in. *Warriors* tells you to swim out to meet it. Don't leave your destiny up to chance. Make a choice—be a warrior!

—*Meadowlark Lemon*

There is a war going on today for the lives of the younger generation. Young people are wandering aimlessly without a sense of purpose or destiny for their lives. I believe this book answers the questions we all have about the condition of our world and its future.

*Warriors* challenges men, young and old alike, to "stand for the truth at all costs," to become the leaders they are called to be and to rise to the real standard of manhood—Christlikeness.

—*Ricky Skaggs*

*Warriors* is a foundational book that lays out a biblical pattern of how to please God as a young man. Fathers, whether your son is thirteen or thirty, this book will be one of your best investments into his life.

—*Bill McCartney*

I met Tom Sirotnak while I was a student at the University of Washington. Having known him for the past six years, I can tell you that Tom lives what he preaches. His desire is to see young men and women fulfill the destiny God has for each of their lives. That vision has produced *Warriors*. I encourage you to read it.

—*Mark Brunell*
*Jacksonville Jaguars*

I encourage every young man and minister to read *Warriors* by Tom Sirotnak. I have had the privilege of knowing Tom behind the scenes, and I can honestly tell you that he is a young man that lives what is written in this book.

*Warriors* is an outpouring of his life. I have seen it at work in his own life, and many of the principles in this book have changed my life and affected the Power Team's lives. I would encourage every young man to get this book and read it—and know that the author lives what he preaches.

—*John Jacobs, Founder*
*The Power Team*

Tom Sirotnak's book, *Warriors*, charges us to step out of mediocrity, fear, and insecurity to fight for our God-given destiny. I know Tom. God uses him to help build godly men, warriors that are willing to put God's principles into operation . . . to live a fruitful, Christian life.

The world is waiting for role models, leaders, and champions, filled with the word of God, to lead us to fulfill our purpose as destined by God. I recommend that you read this book.

—*Rosey Grier*

The call of God is upon this generation, . . . *Warriors* is a book that calls men to reach their full potential for God. *Warriors* has motivated me to strive for nothing short of excellence in my walk with Christ. The call is clear; the mission is certain. It's up to you to choose to be one of God's warriors.

—*Christopher Singleton*
*San Francisco Giants*

*Warriors* should be read by every man in America. Finally, in a clear, bold, unashamed way the truth is recorded. America needs "real men" with "real lives" and "real goals" to be "real examples" for the generations to follow. We need to get this book in the hands of our men so God can get these truths into their hearts.

—*Dr. Forrest Lowry, Senior Pastor*
*Spring Baptist Church, Spring, Texas*

In a day and age of misunderstanding of who and what a real man is, Tom Sirotnak stands as a shining example of a godly man. His life is an example of how men can stand up for what is right without compromising. He teaches men, young and old, how to be warriors for Christ, even in a decadent society. Men are drawn by his strength and his unconditional love and acceptance of them. *Warriors* will inspire each man to take his rightful place as a man for the twenty-first century.

—*Bill Burnett, Pastor*
*Trinity Christian Center*

Radical, confrontational Christianity! Joel 3:9 is an end-time call to wake up the mighty men and declare war. Tom Sirotnak challenges the young men of this generation to rise up to take their place as true *warrior men* in a life-changing, total surrender to the lordship of Jesus. Multitudes of men in our society have surrendered their manhood to "Peter Pan" frivolity and irresponsibility. They are without purpose and passion for any lasting values so they have become aimless, self-serving, and a self-destructive generation. As Tom so vividly points out, only with unwavering, militant commitment to the cause of Christ and biblical ethics can men retake their place of leadership and destiny.

—*Dr. Gary L. Greenwald, Pastor*
*Eagle's Nest Ministries, Irvine, California*

Tom not only states lucidly the mindset of young men today, but offers sound and practical solutions using biblical truths. It's an exciting book to read. You'll be stirred!

—*Dick Mills*
*Dick Mills Ministries, Orange, California*

Tom Sirotnak lays God's standard on the line from the start and challenges young men to meet that standard head on, "The measure of manhood is Jesus Christ." Jesus Christ is truth and real men stand on the truth of Christ. As Tom says, "Christlikeness and manhood go together."

Real men are a dying breed in our world today. Tom is out to stop man's extinction. . . .Tom shoots down the theories and ideas that the world offers and proves that real men follow the Lord Jesus Christ! I've personally heard his powerful testimony about his life as a young college football stud. Now young men all over can receive wisdom from this man after God's own heart.

—*Gene Jennings, Pastor*
*First Baptist Church, Bath, South Carolina*

*Warriors* is **dynamite**! It's a rite of passage into godly manhood. You may have been born a male, but you must choose to be a man. . . . You owe it to yourself to sow the seeds of greatness by reading this book. Dare to be one of God's warriors to your generation.

—*Rich Wilkerson*
*Rich Wilkerson Ministries, Tacoma, Washington*

At a time when a generation of young men struggles to find their uniqueness and identity in a maze of current fads, it is refreshing to read someone who not only analyzes the dilemma but shows a way out!

—*Dr. James D. Marocco, Senior Pastor*
*First Assembly of God, Maui, Hawaii*

God is looking for men of stature, courage, and purpose! *Warriors* challenges young men to be the leaders of their generation. Will you join me in being a warrior for Christ?

—*Reggie White*

The Bible says, "Without a vision, a man perishes." We are all born into the world with God-given skills and abilities. It's up to use to develop these skills and abilities to achieve and fulfill our destiny. Dedicated to all who have influenced and blessed my life.

- To my wife, Dana, who believed in me and is a constant source of encouragement, I reaffirm my undying love. And for our two sons, Stephen Rice and Thomas James, Jr., and for those yet to come (Lord willing, Cody Edward and Sharon Rose), who will carry on the mission and fulfill the call of Christ in their generation. Go for it!

- To my brothers on the Power Team: Rico, Kenan, Shawn, Mark, Jeff, Berry, "The Gripper" Eddie, Craig, Mike, Brandon, and Keith; and John Jacobs, with whom I have shared "Jonathan and David" types of relationships. Your labor will be rewarded.

- To Al Manamtam, my closest brother in Christ who is with me through thick and thin. Our destinines are inseparately interwoven. Keep building the kingdom! You have been born for "such a time as this."

- To Nick Gough, a friend who sticks closer than a brother. We grew up together, then went to USC, got saved, and entered full-time service to Christ together. You are a loyal friend, anointed minister, and constant source of inspiration.

- To all my brothers and sisters at Morning Star Ministries International, my hat is off to you for your bold, daring, and sacrificial profession of faith as you carry out your vision of training leaders to impact the world for God's glory.

- To Mom and Dad, Gloria and Ed, who invested their lives (and food, a lot of food) into me and gave selflessly so I could be what I am today.

- To my father- and mother-in-law, Robert and Joan Cody, who have always been there for our family.
  I thank God for each and every one of you.

—*Tom Sirotnak*
*Anaheim, California*

# CONTENTS

# FOREWORD

IT WAS JOB WHO SAID, "Just as my mouth can taste good food, so my mind tastes truth when I hear it" (Job 12:11, TLB). He did not know that centuries later another would teach that truth is the criterion of spirituality.

When you base your life on truth, the better will be your way and the greater life you will have. Truth is the foundation for both the way and the life.

As you read Tom's book you will discover that he is a lover of truth.

Scripture says, "It is senseless to pay tuition to educate a rebel who has no heart for truth" (Prov. 17:16, TLB). In the university, Tom was the epitome of the rebel who didn't know who he was; but when he found the truth, that gave him the freedom to be the man he has become today. That's why his book is filled with what he has learned and lived in becoming one of God's champions.

He is as bold and fearless in his writing as he is in his preaching. Wrestling bears, punching out cement blocks, lifting ponderous weights, blowing up water bottles, or tearing up thick telephone books is his public persona. But in private he is ever the humble and earnest seeker of God's truth.

"To learn you must be willing to be taught," is the way the Book of Proverbs states it in 12:1 (TLB). The willingness to learn is exhibited in practice. Some people hear. Others do.

There is a vast difference between being a convert and a disciple. This is true not only in Christianity, but in everything in life. A convert listens, but a disciple does — does what he knows is true no matter what the personal cost. There is always a price to pay in leadership. Involvement costs little, while commitment can cost everything.

Tom has paid a great price to bring you the truths in this book. But it is nothing to compare with the price Christ paid to bring the truth to Tom.

Read and learn. Then just do it.

*—Edwin Louis Cole*
*Founder and President*
*Christian Men's Network*
*Dallas, Texas*

# ACKNOWLEDGMENTS

F EW BOOKS ARE SOLELY THE PROVINCE of the author. Such is the case with *Warriors*. The men listed here have all had an impact on my teaching. I have tried to acknowledge their contributions to this book in the notes. Yet what they have taught me is so ingrained in my consciousness that sometimes it is difficult to separate their thoughts from mine.

Most of all, this book is a tribute to Edwin Louis Cole and his Christian Men's Network. Dr. Cole, you have fathered me in masculinity and inspired me as an author. More importantly, you received me as a son. Your spirit of faith, and your message that Christ-likeness and manhood are synonymous, echo throughout this book. I could not have written this book without the years of teaching you invested in me.

Phil Bonasso, my pastor, discipler, and trusted friend, you believed in me and hung in there when no one else did. You have sacrificed and given to me well beyond the call of duty. Like a rider in the saddle, you have molded, shaped, and guided me in Christian maturity. I owe you my life!

I don't have anything that was not invested in me by mighty men. Foremost are Rice Broocks and Greg Ball, who instilled in me a pursuit for holiness, a relentless zeal for souls, and an unashamed boldness for the cause of Christ. I thank both of you for having the courage to challenge me to be all I could be for God. A. C. Green is known across the country as a talented basketball player. "Ace," to me you are an example of selfless giving and incredible courage in standing up to resist the evil forces that plague our world. You are a true warrior of faith.

I also want to give special acknowledgement to Ken Walker, who labored with me in writing this book. God truly knit our hearts together. You literally have captured the heart of my ministry, Victory Network. You masterfully helped sculpt a work that will influence many men. I am honored to have you on my team.

Men, you have all been such a blessing to me and my family. These few paragraphs cannot possibly do justice or speak to the fullness of what you mean to me. Thank you all.

# THE BATTLE
# FOR A GENERATION

*We're street smart, David Letterman clever,*
*  whizzes at Nintendo.*
*We can name more beers than presidents.*
*Pop culture is, to us, more attractive than education.*
*I don't think we can do this dance much longer . . . .*

*—Daniel Smith-Rowsey* [1]

F ROM BEHIND THE PODIUM, I GAZED OUT at the collection of muscle-clad, well-trained bodies. I recognized many of the skilled athletes attending this national conference. I had admired them playing various sports around the country, either live in the stadium or on television. Who was I to address these household names? Me, a one-time third-stringer at the University of Southern California (USC), with limited playing time (and success) on the football field. I had to overcome this psychological intimidation if I were to deliver a Christian message that could reach these modern-day heroes—strong men on the outside, yet desperately wanting to grow spiritually on the inside.

One question burned on my lips. I held back momentarily. Then, with a bold urgency and depth of conviction in my voice, I cried out: "I just want to know one thing from you men!"

A hush came over the crowd.

"I just want to know," I said as I pointed at them, "if you have the guts* to serve Jesus Christ."

Shock jumped out of hundreds of pairs of eyes. They had never expected such a sharp statement to come out of an evangelist's mouth. Nonetheless, the weight of that question struck deep inside their hearts. Some looked shyly at the ground. "Being a man" had never been put so forcefully.

"Men, you have a 'pump' on the outside of your bodies," I continued. "But do you have a spiritual pump on the inside? Deuteronomy 23:1 says, 'No one who is emasculated, or has his male organ cut off, shall enter the assembly of the Lord.' The problem in our society is that we have a bunch of spiritual eunuchs running around, men who have been emasculated by sin. They're living a life of regret because they've compromised their convictions. They've sunk in the muck and mire of peer pressure and have denied the name of Jesus Christ by their lifestyles. We need a new breed of men to stand up in the midst of a wicked and perverted generation, men who will unashamedly proclaim the way of the Lord."

Suddenly, whoops and hollers broke the silence. A host of "amens" and cheers arose from these men as they realized who they are in Christ. They saw the truth: A Christian is not some wimpy, timid nerd who cowers in the face of conflict and constantly runs away from confrontation.

God is raising up such a new breed of men—whether they are athletes, soldiers, doctors, lawyers, business owners, writers, teachers or whatever occupation you care to name—for service in His army. Young men who remain unblemished by the world. Those who are bold in their faith and willing to lay down their lives for Jesus. These men are not afraid to give their all to preach and live

(*Speaking in the vernacular of the locker room I knew from college and professional athletics, I used a cruder word than the one described above.)

the gospel under the power of the Holy Spirit. *Warriors* is a challenge. Men, whether you're young and single, married and just starting a family, or trying to correct your life after a string of mistakes, I call on you to rise up and be the godly leaders our world so desperately needs. If you gain nothing else from this book, remember this: Manhood and Christ-likeness are synonymous.

It's time to raise up modern-day giants of faith, men like Daniel, Joseph, David, and Jeremiah. You may recognize these names from the Bible. But did you realize they were all in their teens when God called them into ministry? As Daniel 11:32b says, "But the people who know their God will display strength and take action."

It is time to locate the men who will dare to obey the call of God in their lives and dare to do great exploits for our King. We must sound the battle cry, assembling young men to stand and give God the best years of their lives for His glory. If you're ready, I'll lead you forward.

Note: As you go through this book, study questions will be included at the end of each chapter. They are geared to stimulate growth and shape you into the man God intends you to be. Your first assignment is to buy a notebook so you can record your answers to the study questions.

Writing them down will help you see where you have come from and where you are going. This will help you remember the information as you chart your destiny. Take the advice of Habakkuk 2:2-3. Write the vision down so you will know what you are pursuing.

# 1

## THE INVISIBLE MAN

*The brave new world has faded, and materialism is back.*
*Status, for teens, centers around money and possessions . . .*
*For boys, the ascetic look of the flower child is out.*
*Muscles are a must; otherwise,*
*you're a "nerd," a "geek," or a "wimp."*

—*American Demographics*[1]

THE MEASURE OF MANHOOD IS JESUS CHRIST. Sound crazy? Sissy? Wimpy? Like so many Christians you know? That's what I used to think. But I learned otherwise by seeking fulfillment in other ways. Striving to find acceptance in the world, I sought to become the image of the rough, tough, macho man. At the end of my quest, I felt confused and defeated. A weak-kneed, spineless jellyfish, my bulging muscles on the outside covered up deep insecurities on the inside.

A chubby, slow, uncoordinated youngster, I grew up desperately seeking the approval of other kids. Though often jeered for my clumsy, slow-footed ways, my size worked to my advantage when I started putting my efforts into sports, especially football. But my red-letter day in elementary school came when I took on the toughest kid in our class.

Out on the playground, I made this bully mad. He came running full speed in my direction. Actually, I didn't stand up to him. He scared me to death. I trembled in my shoes; when he swung, I ducked. He missed, and his momentum sent him flying over me. Without realizing what I was doing, in the same motion I stood up and caught him with my shoulder. The impact tossed him several feet in the air. He landed flat on his back. Dusting himself off, he got up slowly and quietly slumped away to Mama, tears running down his cheeks.

Suddenly I was the new school hero. Though my success was a complete fluke, I thought, "Hey, look at the acceptance I got through fighting this guy." That launched my new search for the physical, "macho he-man" lifestyle. I avidly pursued building up my body to ultra-tough proportions. I thought being a man meant someone so physically intimidating that *nobody* would mess with him. I wanted to look so tough not a soul would dare challenge me to a fight—and if he was foolish enough, I would be able to make mincemeat of him. It may sound simplistic to trace all my actions to a grade school fight with a bully. But that was the turning point that set me on the path of "bigger means better."

Years later I arrived at the USC boasting a 20-inch neck, 20-inch arms and a 54-inch chest. Onlookers gaped whenever I bench-pressed 470 pounds. I also used my physique to land a job as a bar bouncer, where I brawled regularly. When I got really mean, I rubbed men's faces up against stucco walls or chain-link fences.

I amazed people with my physical stunts. On three occasions I wrestled bears standing as tall as 7 feet, 4 inches and weighing 650 pounds. It was all a show, but my willingness to enter the ring impressed the fraternity brothers who talked big but weren't too willing to back it up. I meant to show them that I was the roughest, toughest, most fearless dude on campus. When I got drunk I would run into four-by-four, wooden stop signs and knock them over with a loud crack. One night we went crazy; a bunch of guys dared me to knock down ten "no parking" signs within two blocks. I did it, grinning. Why not? I thought I was the ultimate man.

Even though I never started, and mainly warmed the bench, I was still one of the few walk-ons to stick with the varsity at USC. My willingness to mix it up with future National Football League (NFL) stars like Marcus Allen and Keith Van Horn earned more admiration in my social circles. Because of perseverance, determination, and sacrifice, I earned the honor of being named team captain for one game as a senior.

Besides persevering in football, I belonged to a great fraternity, Theta Xi, which brought access to two of my primary dreams in life: great parties and lots of sorority sisters. Plus, I was on my way to earning a marketing degree from a dynamic business school. Such status earned me a good reputation among my peers. At parties my legend grew. Once I won the beer-chugging contest by downing a sixteen ounce mug in 1.9 seconds.

## Empty Inside

I did these things to win friends and gain attention. But instead of bringing rewards, I felt unfulfilled. My lifestyle covered up the insecurities, fear, and failures gnawing at me. I wanted to be a man *so bad.* The truth was, I didn't know how. Even with all my physical exploits and status on campus, I was bankrupt inside. There was a huge void inside of me—one only God could fill. One night I lay in bed at the fraternity house and thought about the show I was putting on to cover up the truth. Shaking my head and rubbing my eyes, I thought, *Tom, you're such a wimp.*

As time passed, this void expanded through a steady diet of lust, pornography, and immoral relationships. I didn't realize how such stuff strips a man of purpose and responsibility. It made me feel even weaker. Ironically, while I was partying away my college years, I called myself a Christian and belonged to a campus ministry. Finally, when USC made it to the Fiesta Bowl my senior year, things began to change.

Upset over the hypocrisy and inconsistencies that plagued me, I aimlessly wandered the streets of Phoenix. Fortunately, one of my teammates, Mark Boyer, who went on to play in the NFL with the New York Jets, invited me to a Christian gathering. The speaker was former Los Angeles Ram and Hall of Fame member Rosey Grier. Seeing through my counterfeit faith, he challenged me to get the sin out of my life. The night he spoke I felt like laser beams were shooting out of his eyes and resting on me. He said that the only way to serve God was to quit compromising. The words stung as though one of those wooden stop signs had bounced up off the ground and smacked me square in the nose.

As "fate" had it (there is no such thing, the Lord arranged it), Rosey also spoke the following week at USC. He introduced me to Phil Bonasso, who is now my pastor, and Rice Broocks, an evangelist who spoke that night. Afterwards, Phil and Rice counseled with me until I saw that I had never understood what it meant to be a disciple of Jesus Christ. I saw that Jesus was not 100 percent in control of my life. From studies to athletics, work, social life, and family, He must be "Lord of all or not at all." That's when I repented, and God's power changed me. The void in my life vanished. For the very first time, I felt like a whole person. A real man.

## The Missing Man

Our generation faces an environmental disaster worse than the loss of silver-back gorillas, giant pandas, or killer whales. I am referring to the systematic extinction of the human species known as the "masculine man." In modern America's feminist-influenced society, masculinity and manhood have become dirty words. As it is with so many things, I don't believe the extremists speak for the majority of women. Yet their stranglehold on the media and popular entertainment magnifies their influence far beyond reality.

Women's liberation sprang up as a rejection of men's double standards and woeful ignorance of their responsibilities. But over the past two decades, feminism has degenerated into a rebellion (unleashed with much sound and fury) that seeks to eliminate manhood. What has evolved from this movement? A generation with confused sexual roles. This bewilderment produces hard women and soft men.

A letter written to Ann Landers years ago illustrates the feminization of men that has been going on for a long time. Under the headline, "Masculine Men Have Been a Dying Breed," the writer told how his mother ran their family. His dad was a wimp, he lamented, and if anyone was responsible for his weak self-image, it was his father. The author went on to say that almost all his teachers, beginning in the nursery and going through high school, were women.

"The male teachers were all effeminate," he wrote. "In school, the only male employee was the janitor. I was disciplined and rewarded exclusively by women. I learned early where the power was and I wanted to be on the winning side."[2]

In his excellent book, *Missing from Action*, W. M. Hardenbrook said, "When I speak of feminization, I am referring to a conditioning process in modern American culture in which men have been trained to respond to people and situations that are more akin to historical female behavior patterns than they are to historical male behavior patterns."[3]

Irresponsible males who lack conviction and suffer from the Peter Pan syndrome further this loss of masculinity. These are males who reason primarily from their emotions, never want to grow up, never want to accept responsibility for their actions, and don't possess the courage to become the men that God has called them to be.

This Peter Pan syndrome affects many high school and college-age men. I know. I see them constantly on America's campuses. Many of these males have the emotional stability of a roller coaster. Swinging from highs to lows, their decision-making ability is weak and fickle.

## Peter Pan's Failure

The worst thing about the Peter Pan syndrome is its creation of high school and college graduates who are ill-prepared to master anything. The only thing these men cling to is fear: cold, dark dread of unexpected social, mental, and financial pressures. Former Secretary of Education William Bennett has said that never before has a generation of American teens been less healthy, cared for, or prepared for life than their parents when they were at the same age.

A national study released a few years ago by the Times Mirror Center for the People and Press portrayed a generation of young adults (18–29) who are indifferent toward public affairs. It said today's young generation knows less and cares less about its leaders and institutions, and votes less than young people in the past.

I call them the "educated ignorant." Though technologically sophisticated and intelligent, they are emotionally insecure and double-minded. They have no real sense of direction or meaningful philosophy of life. Childish men, inflated with pride, infantile in understanding, disposition, reasoning, and emotion, they are no more fit to rule than a babe in a cradle.

This type of underdeveloped male will rule with all the folly, fickleness, and forwardness of a mere child. Never wanting to grow up, Peter Pans seek escapist lifestyles. Fleeing all pressures and responsibilities, they become easily seduced and intoxicated by pleasure: sex, drugs, alcohol, entertainment, parties, shopping, and sleep.

In the 1950s, the average age of maturity for a man—defined as one who could hold down a job, marry, and provide for his family—was sixteen. During high school in the late seventies, my instructors in a career development class tabbed this average age of maturity as occurring at twenty-six. In a *Los Angeles Times* article in the mid-eighties, one psychologist listed this figure as coming anywhere between the ages of thirty-five and forty. It is frightening to think where men stand in the 1990s.

Unfortunately, Hollywood has contributed substantially to this annihilation of manhood. W. M. Hardenbrook wrote that Hollywood's old macho image portrayed America as a land built by God, guts, and guns. Sadly, the new macho image leaves God out of the equation. "The new macho hero in cinema may demonstrate bravery," he wrote, "but with the unfeeling soul of a robot. He doesn't cry, whine, complain or worry. He only sweats. The male movie goer applauds the screen hero, only to return home with a sense of greater impotence."[4]

During the 1970s and 1980s, the anti-hero syndrome working in our society, due largely to incidents such as the Vietnam War and Watergate, killed off noble heroes with any sense of courage, duty, and righteousness . . . not to mention men who were patriots. The new stars produced by cinema and television were violent, rebellious, emotionless, and sex-crazed. Morality gave way to insanity.

To make matters worse, in countless situation comedies today, TV fathers play bumbling idiots, marriage brims with warfare, and women are mere sex objects. A new species of man has developed from this trend: *Wimps: Made in America!* In essence, such men are insecure, inferior, dull, and inadequate to cope with life. They are shallow, unstable, and immature. We have discarded the strong masculine hero—daring, bold, courageous and a strong leader—for the new, improved, sensitive model—a man who cares more about who he offends than who he protects.

## Lacking Leadership

This country is staggering through a leadership crisis. The times demand bold men of character who are not afraid of proclaiming the Lord's ways in the midst of a wicked, perverted society. Everywhere, whether in business, politics, or education, people are crying out, "Will somebody please take the lead?" Or, as Psalm 94:16 asks, "Who will take his stand for me against those who do wickedness?"

Men are the foundational strength of any government. From the family to the work force to public affairs, as the men of a nation go, so goes the nation. Legendary French Prime Minister Charles de Gaulle summed it up when he said: "Nothing great will ever be achieved without great men, and they are great only if they determine to be so."[5] In essence, as TV host Ben Kinchlow says, "Being male is a matter of birth. Being a man is a matter of choice."[6]

During the 1992 Winter Olympics, I shuddered as one athlete bragged about his philosophy: "I live for the thrills, sex, drugs, and rock 'n' roll. People wish they could live like me, but they don't have the courage." Well, since when does it take courage to live an impure, immoral lifestyle? Standing up against peer pressure, that takes guts. Daring to be a role model by doing what is right in the sight of a holy God. That requires bravery. How many men do you see doing that? Courage stands out from the crowd instead of bowing to it.

This mockery of God's principles for living has brought us to a national moral—and economic—crisis. The words Isaiah wrote thousands of years ago still apply today. Chapter 24, verses 5–6, say, "The earth is also polluted by its inhabitants, for they transgressed laws, violated statutes, broke the everlasting covenant. Therefore, a curse devours the earth, and those who live in it are held guilty. Therefore, the inhabitants of the earth are burned, and *few men are left*" (italics added).

God has placed in the heart of every man the deep, burning desire to be a hero, a champion, a conqueror, an overcomer. Men don't want to be timid, cowardly souls, afraid what might happen if they take a stand for God. They want to stand up, do what is right, and achieve greatness. That is leadership by example instead of seeking out the latest polling data before you make up your mind about what to do.

I saw this truth demonstrated one time during a campus ministry leadership conference. A short, rather ordinary looking evangelist approached the platform with a black bandana around his forehead and a toy AK-47 gun in his hand. Grabbing the microphone in his free hand, he barked, "I believe in the heart of every skinny little preacher is a Rambo just waiting to emerge!" The audience roared with approval.

Months later I assembled some of the Christian football players and students on the USC campus for a prayer meeting. We named it the R.A.M.B.O. Club, which stood for Radically Active Men on Biblical Offensive. Looking into each of their eyes, I said, "I'm here to punch your RAMBO button." In the heart of each of those men was a spiritual RAMBO. Some of them have gone on to do great things in the Lord's service.

Men desire to be a hero. In recent years the world has warred against this type of thought. Critics sneer, "Oh, you just have a big ego and you want to feed it." Men, I'm here to say that God designed you with that ego. Not to exalt yourself or act like some macho "stud" but so He can provoke you to do great exploits for His glory.

Having an ego is natural. It should be, since it's a gift from God. We see the ideal man as the hero. Women dream of a knight in shining armor who will appear at the right moment and whisk them off to safety. The same with young children, who are always eager to brag, "My dad can whip your dad" or "No one is as good as my dad." In today's divorce-filled climate, there are also the kids who cry, "I just wish I had a dad." Strong men, our society needs you!

### What's a Real Man?

This is one of my favorite questions as I visit high school and college campuses around the United States. The standard responses fall into four categories:

- Physical—who's the "biggest" or "toughest."

- Drinking—who can chug down a six-pack of beer the fastest.

- Social—who is the most influential.

- Sexual—who can "score" the most with the ladies.

Others believe a real man is someone who does whatever he wants to do, or a guy who has mastered financial independence.

Such answers remind me of a couch potato who has overdosed on Rambo movies. None of the above qualities even remotely resembles the image of a true man. Psalm 101:6 says, "I will make the godly of the land my heroes" (TLB). What's the point? *The real standard of manhood is someone who will stand for the truth at all costs.*

During the heyday of the Vietnam War protests, a college student resisted a hostile mob intent on burning the American flag. Physically guarding the flag pole, he declared, "You are not going to defame the flag for which my father died." It wasn't his size that intimidated that crowd. It was because he stood for a symbol of freedom and truth.

Likewise, for the Christian, Jesus says, "I am the way, and the truth, and the life" (John 14:6). When the Christian man takes a stand for the gospel of the kingdom of God, he has fixed himself in support of the ultimate in truth. That is who Jesus is: *the Truth.*

So many people equate being a Christian with a weakling, a wimp. One night while I was preaching on a college campus, a student yelled, "Jesus is a crutch!" I replied, "You're right. What's yours? Alcohol? Women? Fame? We are all trusting in something. But will it support your lifestyle or lead you straight to hell?"

If Christianity is a crutch, then give me two. I desperately need Jesus to guide my life. Without Him, it was headed straight down the tubes. Is yours aimed downward? Let's look at how to avoid that.

### Gut Check

1. Define your strengths. Write them out.

2. Define your weaknesses—morals, ethics and habits. Write them out. What are some of your insecurities? Do you need others' approval? Why?

3. In Psalms and Proverbs, pick out five to ten positive verses that represent what you are seeking. For example, if you need wisdom and knowledge, claim Proverbs 1:7, "The fear of the Lord is the beginning of knowledge; fools despite wisdom and instruction." If you've never known a father's love, proclaim in the words of Psalms 68:5 that God is "a father of the fatherless." Offer these verses up as prayers and watch God mold and shape you into a man of good character.

4. Who are your heroes? Why do you admire them? What godly traits do they have?

5. As you look at biblical characters like Moses, Joseph, David, Peter, and Paul, what traits of their personalities are similar to yours? What can you learn from them?

# 2

## YOUTH:
## PASSAGE INTO MANHOOD

*The problem in this nation is not with the prostitutes, the punks (and) the pushers. But it's with puny, pampered, passive preaching from the pulpits of America ... Nobody, it seems, is standing and preaching that the Word of God is the Word of God and hell is hot and heaven is high and sin is wrong and God and marriage are right. It's time to take a stand.*

*—Pastor Bobby Boyles[1]*

STANDING UP AND BECOMING A MAN. It sounds simple. But it's not. When I played nose guard at USC, the coach called his defensive line his gorillas. We prided ourselves on being the meanest, toughest men in all of college football.

Once I bragged to some high school students: "We were so mean that we wouldn't just sack the quarterback. We would rip his arm off and then go up into the stands to find his parents and beat them over the head with their son's arm!" One of the nation's top teams, our physical intimidation caused some opponents to tip off their plays. The telltale sign: when they broke from their huddle, three backs were laughing and the fourth was pale as a ghost.

Of course, such talk was all a joke. But the football players loved to tell such stories. The crowds ate it up and it helped "psych" the team up on Saturday afternoons. We may have been kidding around during the week, but the more we prided ourselves on being big, bad, and bold, the better we played after the kickoff.

One day during practice warm-ups, the coach looked around at his gorillas and yelled, "Hey, we don't have any of those faggot Christians on this team, do we?" Not one person raised his voice in objection. Not only was I afraid to say anything, I knew given my hypocritical lifestyle, any response would have provoked howls of laughter. So, that day no real man stood up. We may have owned bulging biceps, but in size of spirit we were timid, scared weaklings.

## Becoming a Man

Let's return to the basic question of this book: "What makes a real man in our generation?" There's an old saying that goes, "You're not a man until your father says so." Where does that leave so many young men who have never had a dad at home? Or, if he does, fails to present a godly example?

In our society the primary rite of passage to manhood seems to be how quickly we lose our virginity. Locker room stories of sexual exploits and adulterous relationships often shape our opinions. Yet this sort of activity does not make a real man. In truth, it is the exact opposite. Still, this view prevails because so many young men grow up in fatherless homes. Staggering numbers of marriages end in divorce. While there are quarrels over the statistics, the fact remains that millions of young boys and girls grow up lacking the father that they need. (They need a mother just as much. Proper parenting is the joint responsibility of a man and woman.)

While there have been changes in recent years with increasing numbers of fathers seeking custody of their children, the norm has been for the father to leave, with the mother raising the children. This leaves a void of masculine influence that is necessary for all children, boys or girls. Boys especially need a godly, masculine role model to emulate.

Take former major league baseball star Bo Jackson, who also used to chew up yardage for the Los Angeles Raiders. In his book, he recalled how he never had enough food at home, but he could beat on the other kids and steal their lunch money to get something to eat. "But I couldn't steal a father," he said. "I couldn't steal a father's hug when I needed one. I couldn't steal a father's———— whipping when I needed one."[2]

When Orlando Magic center Shaquille O'Neal released his rap album, "Shaq-Fu: The Return" in the fall of 1994, he dedicated a song on it to his stepfather. In it, he tells how his biological father never bothered to help him grow up. It was his stepfather who took him from a boy to a man, he said. O'Neal's heartfelt tribute also shows how important a father is to a young man's personal, cultural, and social development. This need does not stop with boys. Girls may struggle with their feminine identity when there is no available contrast in role models.

Even in traditional families where both parents are present, many boys lack an example of manhood's virtues. There are millions of fathers so preoccupied with work that they spend only a few minutes a day focusing on their children. Others are physically or mentally abusive. For some, their sins are not ones of commission, but omission. In other words, it's not what they have done that hurts; it's what they failed to do. These are the fathers who are apathetic and disinterested in the activities of their children. Then there are the drug and alcohol abusers who destroy the image of a loving father. It's one of the greatest blocks in American society to people accepting God as their loving Father. The only father image they know makes them run from the very word.

If you are a victim, there is hope. Despite your suffering, the Lord promises that if you will forgive your father and release him (by an act of your will) from his sins, God will heal you. He will cure your past hurts, cleanse your heart of hatred, and  personally guide you into the fullness of manhood. Psalm 27:10 promises, "For my father and my mother have forsaken me, but the Lord will take me up." In Psalms 68:5, He's called a "father of the fatherless."

If it hasn't happened already, today is the day He is looking you in the eye. With the firmness of a man, and all compassion and love in His heart, Jesus is saying to you, "My son, welcome into manhood. Today you can find acceptance from your Heavenly Father. "If I am for you, who can be against you?"

Jesus Christ and the power of His cross to change our lives represents is our rite of passage into godly masculinity. This type of man is under God's control and shows the fruits of His Spirit, such as love, joy, peace, patience, and goodness. Ephesians 4:13 says, "Until we all attain to the unity of the faith, and the knowledge of the Son of God, to a *mature man*, to the measure of the stature which belongs to the *fulness of Christ*" (italics added).

Remember what I said in the introduction? Christ-likeness and manhood go together! Ephesians 4:14–15 continues, "As a result, we are no longer to be children . . . but speaking the truth in love, we are to grow up in all aspects into Him."

## Grow Up, Young Man

The ability to stand in the face of adversity is one measure of manhood. Just as young boys want to see the manly role model lived out before them at home, the number one desire of a father is to see his son grow up and become a man. Likewise, every son's number one desire is to hear his father's affirmation that he is a man.

This reality appears in 1 Kings 2:1–3. We read in verses 1–2: "As David's time to die drew near, he charged Solomon his son, saying, 'I am going the way of all the earth. Be strong, therefore, and show yourself a man.'"

When death draws near and wisdom comes forth for the benefit of future generations, it is a profound moment. Truth comes forth at a man's final moment of departure, to leave an inheritance of wisdom for future generations. This is the most important legacy a man can leave. . . not his money. What good will a million dollars do your children if you never teach them how to manage it? They'll burn it up faster than a mountain forest fire on a crisp October afternoon.

Ever see the movies, where a criminal who is mortally wounded confesses the who-did-it of his crime? He wants to die with a clean conscience and set the record straight. In a similar vein, this is what is happening in 1 Kings. David wanted to impart his heritage to his son, Solomon, who was in line to inherit the throne. He wanted to pass on the greatest bits of truth he had accumulated during his long life. He wanted his son to be a strong leader, a man, the type of person who would leave a distinguished mark in the future.

In verse three, he told Solomon the secret of manhood, "And keep the charge of the Lord your God, to walk in His ways, to keep His statutes, His commandments, His ordinances, and His testimonies, according to what is written in the law of Moses, that you may succeed in all that you do and wherever you turn."

David assured Solomon that if he would honor God and seek the Lord's ways and always please Him, success would be guaranteed. Later, Solomon testified to this in Ecclesiastes 12:13: "The conclusion, when all has been heard, is: fear God and keep His commandments, because this applies to every person."

Be strong and show yourself a man. That is the challenge. Come out from the world's system, its teachings to glorify self, to "look out for number one" and "do whatever feels good." Dare to be separate and have a heart devoted to the Lord.

Now, daring to be different requires courage. To find it, allow the Heavenly Father's grace to touch you. He will give you the ability to change into the man His Word says you can be—holy and secure in your identity. When you follow His Word, you will be strong, decisive, and consistent.

Jesus is looking to you this day. His first desire as a Father is that you, His son, would grow up. For even "the anxious longing of the creation waits eagerly for the revealing of the sons of God" (Rom. 8:19). Or, as Paul said in 1 Timothy 4:12, "Let no one look down on your youthfulness, but rather in speech, conduct, love, faith and purity, show yourself an example of those who believe."

Did you catch that? Paul exhorted Timothy to show himself a man in five key areas:

1. Reputation

2. Character

3. Morality

4. Ethics

5. Habits

In other words, if Timothy lived the type of life that would lead to a good reputation, demonstrate he had character, was of high morals, was ethical in all his dealings, and maintained good habits, then nobody could look down on him. They would have to consider him a man in every sense of the word.[3]

## Answering the Call

In Ecclesiastes 7:28, Solomon said, "I have found one man among a thousand." Years later, one of America's founding fathers, Benjamin Franklin, observed, "Nine out of ten men are suicides." In other words, most men might as well throw away their lives and be counted as worthless, because they will make no impact on society for good or bad and leave no lasting remembrance.

Godly, masculine men are still a rare breed. Will you be that one man among the thousand who will dare to stand as a man? Or will you cower with the other 999, weak-kneed, Milquetoast, flaky, mama's boys who don't have the guts? Oh, for the one who will stand! The seeds of greatness await to sprout fruit in that person who will impact the world for God's glory!

A.C. Green of the Phoenix Suns is such a man. I remember his rookie season in Los Angeles. Like other rookies, he had to endure constant harassment and practical jokes. As he started to practice one day, a teammate came up to tell him he had a phone call. He told me, "Tommy, I knew if I got that call, I would be late to practice. That phone was a long way away, and if I were late to practice, I'd be in big trouble."

Trouble meant extra laps after practice or being charged with a large fine. But being a naive rookie, he thought, "Well, maybe I'd better get it." Off he ran to answer the call. He picked up the receiver and sure enough, nothing but a dial tone. Running back towards the arena in desperation, hoping to make it to practice in time, A.C. muttered to himself, "They got me. I can't believe it. They got me good."

When he burst through the door, practice had already started. The players laughed, "Ha, ha, ha, look at the rookie!"

"Hey, A.C.," one piped up, "did you get the call?"

"Yeah," he nodded, embarrassed. "I got it all right."

"Oh, yeah, Ace, who called?" prodded a legendary teammate.

After a momentary silence, Green blurted, "It's my Father and He wants to talk to you!" All season long, A.C. told me, he kept going back to that star player to challenge, "Hey, have you answered the call? My Father's still on the line waiting."

That is my question to you. Will you answer the Father's call? Young men, no matter what your age, *right now* is the best time to serve God. Right now, while you are at the prime of your physical strength. Give God the best years of your life and you will be eternally blessed. Don't throw it away in vain pursuits of pleasure.

Youth is not a time to waste your life with foolish experiments, whether with drugs, alcohol, or sex. You don't have time for that. Pursue God, He has a purpose for your life. You owe it to Him to discover the purpose of your existence. Then, throw yourself into it with all your heart.

Let no one look down on your youthfulness. God did not intend for youth to be a blunder, manhood a struggle, or old age a regret. Ecclesiastes 11:9–10 says, "Rejoice, young man, during your childhood, and let your heart be pleasant during the days of young manhood. And follow the impulses of your heart and the desires of your eyes. Yet know that God will bring you to judgment for all these things. So, remove vexation from your heart and put away pain from your body, because *childhood and the prime of life are fleeting*" (italics added).

*The Living Bible* puts it this way in Ecclesiastes 12:1, "Don't let the excitement of being young cause you to forget about your Creator."

Do you dare to answer the call? Then read on.

### Gut Check

1. Describe your relationship with your father. How did he treat you? How do you feel about him? What godly marks of his can you imitate? Write them down.

2. For those who answered question 1 negatively, the Bible commands us to forgive even as Jesus forgave us. This is known as the "principle of release." We cannot be released from our fears,

insecurities, and pain without releasing those who have harmed us. Remember, forgiveness lies in a man's will, not his emotions. If your father injured you on your masculine journey, forgive him—for abusive language, physical abuse, insensitivity, alcoholism, neglect, hard-heartedness, lack of control, or other weakness.

No matter how horrible the cause, you cannot hold on to unforgiveness if you want to be healed. As you release your father of his guilt, Jesus will be your justice, healer, emotional stability, and the redeemer of your youth. He will usher you into maturity as a man of God. Pray the following prayer:

Dear Lord, I ask Your forgiveness for harboring bitterness, hatred, and anger against my father. The Bible says that we are to honor our father and mother that we can enjoy a good life and long days. I don't want my days to be cut short. I don't want my father's sins to live in me. By a decision of my will and through Your grace, I release my father from all guilt, abuse and wrong. Thank you, heavenly Father, that in forgiving my dad, I have become released this day to become the man you want me to be. Through my relationship with You, my past is redeemed, my future in secure and I will find guidance, wisdom and affection through Your Son, Jesus. Amen.

3. God has called men to be His witness and stand up for the cause of Christ. Are you afraid to be identified as a Christian around your family, peers, or business associates?

a. If you answered yes, define your fears. Are you afraid because of:

- Lack of knowledge about your faith?

- Possible intimidation from individuals or the group?

- Shame? Being judged as weak or labeled a wimp?

- Compromise? You would rather "go along" with the world?

List the actions you will take to overcome these fears.

b. If you answered no, tell about your last encounter and the boldness it took to be associated with Christ?

4. How can you be as bold as A. C. Green?

5. What are you doing now that will prepare you for future challenges?

# 3

# SIN:
# AN EQUAL
# OPPORTUNITY KILLER

*Give me a hundred men who fear nothing but sin, and desire nothing but God, and I will shake the world. I care not a straw whether they be clergymen or laymen; such alone will overthrow the kingdom of Satan and build up the kingdom of God on the earth.*

*—John Wesley*
*Colonial era evangelist and founder of the Methodist Church[1]*

EVERY TIME YOU HEAR THE NAME OF JESUS, you face a decision: Jesus or Satan, heaven or hell. Choose this day whom you will serve. Sin. Many wonder if it even exists. Yes, it does. Refusing to follow God's instructions for life so you can follow your selfish desires is wrong. It is sin. You have the choice of what to do, and the road you travel determines the outcome of your life. If you think that sounds like a cliché, let me tell you about the fate of a man who chose not to follow Christ.

While I was serving as a campus ministry evangelist, I visited San Jose State University to help revive a group that had been going stale. During that time, I counseled with Ricky Barry Jr., the star of the basketball team. He was a sure first-round draft pick in the National Basketball Association. After many Bible studies over the period of a month, his heart seemed tender towards God. Nevertheless, he never decided to come under the Lordship of Jesus.

The day before I left to go back to Los Angeles, I saw him in a campus video arcade. Taking my last opportunity to convince him, I said: "Ricky, as of today, you've not made a commitment to Christ. You're going to be a first-round draft pick. You'll have all the success and fame that money can buy. But do you know what you'll find in the NBA without Jesus? Absolutely nothing. You'll be bankrupt on the inside."

He stared back and stood silently for a few moments. Then, sighing softly, he said, "Tom, I'm just not ready yet."

I walked away, sadly shaking my head.

Several months later, I was getting ready to go to bed when I heard this TV bulletin: "Up-and-coming NBA superstar commits suicide." Staying up to watch the late news, I sat in stunned silence when I learned that superstar's identity—none other than Ricky Barry.

What a tragedy! What a difference choosing Jesus would have made to him! I grieved over the loss of this fine young man. This was an all-too-soon end to the life of a man brimming with promise.

Our culture features countless, similar stories of suicide of teens and young people under the age of twenty-five. Considering that, why do so many scoff at the idea that Satan exists? Who else would drive people to take their own life? Do you have any friends who "like" you so much they want you to put a bullet in your head? Of course not! They want to help you get through the difficulty and come out of it claiming the victory. But Satan tries to make you think your present circumstances are impossible, your past too ugly, or your crimes too vicious or too numerous for you to ever amount to anything good.

If he can't do that, he'll try to make you think life is utterly hopeless. Why else would millionaire "grunge music" star Kurt Cobain kill himself? He sang of how he hated himself and wanted to die. And so he did, at the end of a shotgun. Why weren't his fame and fortune enough? Why was he in such deep despair? Among other things, he no doubt felt the same emptiness inside that nagged at Ricky Barry.

Commenting on Cobain's death, Pearl Jam lead singer Eddie Vedder, told of tearing up his hotel room in Washington, D.C. After ripping the room to shreds, he said he felt at home in the rubble. At that moment, it represented his world. People think you are some kind of grand person, he said, just because you can put your feelings into songs. Noting the irony of those who look to musicians for answers, he said: "They write letters and come to the shows . . . hoping we can fix everything for them. But we can't. What they don't understand is that you can't save somebody from drowning if you're treading water yourself."[2]

The one who makes you think you're treading water is Satan. He is your mortal enemy. His plan is to get your eyes off God. Why? Because the Lord has prepared a divine destiny for you. Because the devil opposes everything that God does, he wants to rob you of that divine inheritance and destroy your life. Matthew 7:13–14 warns, "Enter by the narrow gate; for the gate is wide, and the way is broad that leads to destruction, and many are those who enter by it. For the gate is small, and the way is narrow that leads to life, and few are those who find it."

Today, the road map of your life may be bringing you to this crossroads. Will you enter the broad door because it looks wide and easy? Or the narrow one that appears too puritanical, too difficult? Proverbs 8:36 warns, "But he who sins against me injures himself; all those who hate me love death."

Just as the fascinating flicker of fire tempts a moth, so sin—ignoring God's instructions for life to follow your own desires—lures a man. Drawing near, when he gets close enough, he finds destruction. What a contradiction! The world rushes toward hell as though it were heaven, while rejecting heaven as if it were hell.

## The Ultimate Liar

In John 8:44, the Bible calls Satan the father of lies. The devil paints such a pretty picture of what it's like on that wide road. He lures you with thoughts like: "Hey, come on, you can do what you want. Run free without those bothersome restrictions God puts on you. After all, these are the best years of your life. Enjoy things while you're still young. Live it up or you'll miss out on all the fun."

Remember, as the father of all lies, his number one attribute is that of deceiver. His primary motive is to kill you. In John 10:10, Jesus says, "The thief [Satan] comes only to *steal*, and *kill*, and *destroy*." Then He adds, "I came that they might have *life*, and might have it abundantly" (italics added.) Since the fall of Adam and Eve in the Garden of Eden, all men have tasted of the stinging serpent's venom of sin. Left untreated, sin brings eternal death. On earth, it drags you down to depths of great misery. As it is with the devil, so it is with sin. It's a candy-coated poison. It may look appealing and sweet to the taste, but it's like swigging down a pint of poisoned vinegar. While promising to serve and please, sin ultimately dominates your life, leaving you without any choices—other than the sour sensation of death.

When I worked as a bar bouncer, I used to watch sin's destructive effects on people. One night a group of sorority sisters came stumbling up to the bar entrance, laughing and giggling. As they drew closer, I could hear their conversation. It went something like this: "Boy, we had such a blast last night. My boyfriend, Johnny, got so wasted. We were coming downstairs and he threw up all over me!" What fun! Does getting sick and making a fool of yourself sound like a good time? Yet, that is what millions pursue.

Before I repented of my sin, I did the same thing. I drank and partied constantly. I thought sin was fun. So did many of my friends at USC. Like Bret Holman, who was vice president of one of the big fraternities. He came to Southern California from Reno, Nevada. You may envision Reno as a gambling haven and big-time party city, but in comparison to Los Angeles it's a small town. Moving out to the land of surf and sun, Bret had visions of grandeur. He wanted to fit into the fast-paced lifestyle and earn the business degree that would pave the way to financial success.

As happens so often, his thirst for status and social acceptance led him through a slow decline of morals, ethics, and character. This decline never happens overnight. No, it goes an inch at a time, so gradually that you barely notice it taking place. A compromise here, a lie now and then, a big drunk plus a snort of something there, and you're at the bottom of a wasteland. Bret's story follows in his own words.

### The Big Reward

There was a thick blue line that ran down the street from the front door of our frat house, down the sidewalk on fraternity row, and across the street to one of the big local bars. The joke about the blue line was that if you got so "wasted" drunk at the bar, you could always follow the blue line home. It was some joke. Until one night I found myself doing exactly that. That was just one of several times my actions caused me to completely lose control.

The night I pledged (was accepted into) the fraternity I was out with the boys and wanted to prove to them that I could stay with them for as long as they drank. I thought that it would make me look like a real man and gain their approval. That night started the worst nightmare of my life! Not only did I prove to be a "lightweight" drinker, I got so drunk that as we sat at the table, eating and drinking, I began vomiting all over everybody.

They started screaming at me to get out and yelled at one of my pledge brothers to take me home. My poor buddies could barely help me stumble my way back across campus to my dorm room. At one point I even fell into a fountain and almost drowned in two feet of water. Eventually, after getting sicker than I would have imagined in a nightmare, the medical center diagnosed me as suffering from alcohol poisoning.

The next day, with a splitting headache and queasy stomach, I sheepishly made my way back to the fraternity house. I thought for sure my previous night's antics were going to bring my dismissal from this large national fraternity. But to my surprise, not only was I not reprimanded by the leaders, I was the new hero of the house. I found my ungodly actions rewarded instead of frowned on. I was on my way to becoming a party animal and had a reputation to prove it.

After becoming a Christian and looking back on it, I see how foolish I really was. Those so-called friends who loved me while I was a big party animal just loved me because I approved of their ungodly practices. Once I started living for God they ran from me as if I had the plague.

Let me tell you: it's not "cool" being known as a drunk. It's not "rad" to use women for your own pleasure. I thought my party status made me a big man. But the bigger my reputation grew the smaller I felt inside. If you're going to follow the crowd, you better look where they're going. Because you'll end up right there with them.

Many of those whose path I was following now wear labels like "alcoholic," "divorced," "rapist" and "failure." I didn't want to end up like them. I'm so glad I turned my life over to Jesus Christ. He initiated me into real manhood—as a Christian disciple. Now I have a beautiful wife and a sweet baby girl.

I can't imagine missing the joy and freedom of family life and the thrill of following God's destiny for me. I can't believe I almost forfeited all this.

If you have to compromise your values and morals to earn your friends' approval, they really aren't your friends. If you do sell out—you're a wimp. You will live a life of regret, like I almost did. If you are a Christian you don't need anyone's approval except your Heavenly Father's. Experiencing fraternity life, women, and social prosperity sounds so glamorous and thrilling. It seems so "right." But Proverbs 16:25 warns, "There is a way which seems right to a man, but its end is the way of death."

## Drunk as a Skunk

Ed Cole addresses the utterly ridiculous habit of drinking to the point of oblivion. On several occasions I have traveled with the founder of the Christian Men's Network and author of books *Maximized Manhood* and *Strong Men in Tough Times*. During his speaking engagements he calls sin a form of insanity. Generally, the crowd chuckles. Holding up his hand, he says, "Wait a minute. It's true. Isn't it the most insane thing to think that a cool, wet porcelain bowl becomes the greatest source of comfort and security for a man in a drunken state?"

Yet that is typical of the devil's lie. Unfortunately, when you swallow his ideas, you sink to the bottom. That is exactly where Satan wants to lead you. He wants to strip you of all character and morality while luring you into hell. Romans 6:23 plainly states, "The wages of sin is death." Sin is an equal opportunity killer. It doesn't care who you are. Sin is no respecter of fame or status. Sin does not care whether you are young or old, rich or poor. Its effects are deadly.

At a high school assembly designed to address the need for sexual abstinence, a young girl wrote a note that was forwarded to me on stage. She asked, "If I don't know my boyfriend has AIDS and I have sex with him, will I get AIDS?" I thought, "What a poor, naive girl. Does she think that AIDS will ignore her because she didn't know it was there?"

The HIV virus doesn't say, "Oh, I'm so sorry, I'll move on to somebody else. I didn't know you were a movie star. I didn't know you were a famous athlete. I didn't know you were one of the richest people in town. I didn't know you were a teenager with a full, rich life ahead of you." Make no mistake about it. Sin will nail you, whether you know you are sinning or not.

Apart from the blood of Jesus, there is no quick fix solution to immunize you from the deathly sting of sin. It takes a lifetime of vigilance and fighting against the devil's cunning schemes. Lest sin's power overcome us, we must be diligent and faithful to study God's Word and trust in His grace. Then, when trials and temptations assault us, we will know exactly how to respond and preserve our Christian witness.

I remember reading a rather humorous story that illustrates how we need to stand ready to resist sin. If we're not, we can be caught flat-footed without a clue about what to do. This story shows the dangers of living carelessly. It is foolish to think you can stay one step ahead of sin's disastrous effects, somehow beat the odds and never suffer any consequences.

A young soldier who was fighting in Italy during World War II jumped into a foxhole just ahead of some bullets. The soldier immediately tried to deepen the hole for more protection and was frantically scraping away the dirt with his hands. He unearthed something metal and brought up a silver crucifix, left by a former resident of the foxhole. A moment later another leaping figure landed beside him as the shells screamed overhead. When the soldier got a chance to look, he saw that his new companion was an Army chaplain. Holding out the crucifix, the soldier gasped, "Am I glad to see you! How do you work this thing?"[3]

Don't wait until it is too late and your life is nothing more than a mangled mess. There's an old saying that goes, "If you haven't let go of your sins, you're holding on to a hand grenade with the pin pulled out."

## The Knockout Punch

God is doing something great today. Something new. He's calling young men to arise and lead the great sleeping giant known as His church. He's telling us that there is a great "promised land" out there. It's for all of us. This means corporately, as His church, and individually, as His children. Each of you has a divine calling or purpose. This destiny, preordained by God for your life, contains much joy, contentment, and success!

Following Satan's lures is like falling right into a trap. Why else do you think the devil fights so hard to trick people into thinking that when they follow a sin-laden path, they are doing the right thing? Satan opposes God and everything that God does, which is why he hates humans. God created us in His image.

During a campus appearance famed heavyweight boxer Earnie Shavers pointed out how sneaky Satan is. Boxing fans may remember that Shavers won more fights by knockout than any other man in boxing history. As he talked with a group of students, someone asked him about his toughest fight. Given his background, most expected him to talk about climbing into the ring with such heavyweight champions as Muhammad Ali, Ken Norton, or Larry Holmes. In his high, soft, squeaky voice, Earnie stunned everyone with his answer: "Toughest fight, ah. Toughest fight I ever fought was with the devil. He fights dirty, 'cause you can't see him. That's why I'm here talking to you young people now, so that you won't have to go through some of the same pitfalls I did."

Earnie's comments that day demonstrated the same kind of heart God has for us. He left us the Bible's instruction and examples so we would know how to avoid the devil's snares. That day, Earnie made a statement that I'll never forget: "This Bible is God's technique Book. It's a training manual on how to slip life's knockout punches."

Read God's Word and you'll be better prepared to avoid the knockout punch of sin. It comes in five primary forms, which you'll read about in the next chapter.

## Gut Check

1. Is image everything? Is gaining the world worth losing your soul?

2. Describe what happens if you don't confess your sins (see Ps. 32:1–6 and Prov. 8:32).

3. Describe the benefits of serving God.

4. Do you or someone you know like to get "out of control"? What are the long-term consequences from those actions?

5. What do you do when trouble arises?

# 4

## FIVE REASONS YOU WON'T ENTER YOUR PROMISED LAND

*They're resigned to the fact that their tickets are punched but their train is rusted to the rails. They don't expect much, which is why they work so hard to take care of what they've got.*

*—Henry Allen*
*The Washington Post[1]*

A MAN WALKED UP TO ME at an open-air beach rally, mocking me as I preached the gospel. Finally, he sneered, "If God would come down to earth and stand before me, I'd believe in Him." Shaking my head, I answered, "No, you wouldn't. You would more likely fry like a piece of bacon because God's perfect holiness would consume your sin."

A sinful man cannot stand in the presence of a holy God for even one second. If God were to allow a sinner into His kingdom, it wouldn't be perfect anymore. Being a loving God, He doesn't want anyone to perish. The Lord wants everyone to join Him in heaven. But, because He is just, His love cannot override His justice. To solve this dilemma, He sent Jesus to pay the wages of our sin, which was death. In doing so, He provided us the capacity to live holy (meaning set apart, not perfect) lives, even in the midst of peer pressure from a wicked, perverted world.

One of the biggest mistakes people make (including some Christians) is thinking that the Bible is a bunch of stories about old, dried up men that has nothing to do with us today. Wrong! The Bible has everything to do with us today, because we are no different than humans portrayed in biblical history. The Bible is a necessary part of modern life. It's the only book that provides the perfect directions on how to avoid going the wrong direction.

Bear with me in this chapter for some heavy "Bible talk." It's necessary to show you how past mistakes can help you avoid the same blunders in the future. The basis for this teaching[2] comes from 1 Corinthians 10:1–10, where the apostle Paul tells the story of the children of Israel seeking to enter Canaan, the promised land. Canaan flowed with milk and honey. God had sworn to give it to them. Yet, as they stood on the verge of a great blessing, they blew it. Paul recalls the five deadly sins that disqualified them from entering into God's blessings. These are the same five sins that will block you from your rewards.

> For I do not want you to be unaware, brethren, that our fathers were all under the cloud, and all passed through the sea; and all were baptized into Moses in the cloud and in the sea; and all ate the same spiritual food; and all drank the same spiritual drink, for they were drinking from a spiritual rock which followed them; and the rock was Christ.

> Nevertheless, with most of them God was not well-pleased; for they were laid low in the wilderness. Now these things happened as examples for us, that we should not crave evil things, as they also craved. And do not be idolaters, as some of them were; as it is

written, *"The people sat down to eat and drink, and stood up to play."* Nor let us act immorally, as some of them did, and twenty-three thousand fell in one day. Nor let us try the Lord, as some of them did, and were destroyed by the serpents. Nor grumble, as some of them did, and were destroyed by the destroyer.

Did you recognize the five sins? They include:

1. Idolatry

2. Immorality

3. Trying the Lord

4. Craving evil

5. Grumbling

### Idolatry

The key letter in idolatry is "I." I want, I think, I feel. Are you guilty of it? Ask yourself: What do I think about? What do I set my heart on? What do I really want out of life? If it is anything other than to glorify Jesus and establish His purposes, you are following idols.

Idolatry is a value system in which something besides God is considered more worthy of your devotion. Yet, Ezekiel 14:3 plainly says, "Son of man, these men have set up their idols *in their hearts,* and have *put right before their faces* the stumbling block of their iniquity. Should I be consulted by them at all?" (italics added).

Idols compete for our affection for God and block us from undistracted devotion to Him. We can easily become obsessed with them. Like Ezekiel warned, we set them up in front of our faces and look at them so hard we can't see anything else. Idols come in many forms. Americans think if we don't have carved statues or voodoo dolls over the fireplace that we don't worship idols. Wrong! There's money, sports, prestige, power, success, sex, cars, pleasure, and vacations. Anything that consumes our time, attention, and desires.

None of the above are automatically wrong. It takes money to live. Success can be a God-given reward for hard work. We should develop our minds. A vacation can recharge our mentally-drained batteries. However, we can't allow any of these to replace God. It's what we do with what He gives us that makes the difference.

The rich young ruler, whose story appears in the Bible, is an example of a man who misused his God-given talents and material blessings. The passage infers that he was a popular, moral, and deeply religious person. As Jesus sets out on a journey, this sharp, good-looking young man comes running up to ask, "Good Teacher, what shall I do to inherit eternal life?"

Because of the young man's sincerity, Jesus felt a deep love for him. Yet, He knew the young man's idol—money—would prevent him from inheriting God's kingdom. So He said, "One thing you lack: go and sell all you possess, and give to the poor, and you shall have treasure in heaven, and come, follow me" (Mark 10:21).

Jesus knew this man would not follow Him as long as he cherished wealth. The Lord wasn't opposed to this man's riches. Jesus just didn't want him loving money more than God. When His words unmasked the young man's heart, "his face fell, and he went away grieved, for he was one who owned much property" (Mark 10:22). The real irony was that the property owned him.

Phoenix Suns' veteran forward A.C. Green is an example of a man using his talents for the glory of God. Like the rich young ruler, he's been rewarded for his special skill. In Green's case, his life had been enriched by professional basketball. But it hasn't overtaken him. Green uses his money wisely—establishing a youth foundation, funding businesses to help provide inner-city employment and producing a video that spreads the message of abstinence from premarital sex.

I watched him speak to a group of young men one time while he was still playing in Los Angeles. He was quite direct with his message: "I'm not obsessed with professional basketball. That's not who I am, it's just something I do. Basketball doesn't rule my life, Jesus does. I'm not first and foremost an L.A. Laker, I'm a child of God. If you don't see me playing one day, don't worry. Just know I'm out preaching the gospel somewhere."

A.C. has his head in the right place. Too many stars and millions of lesser-known figures pursue idols instead. The problem with idolatry is it promises earthly fulfillment but lacks eternal benefits. Are there idols in your life? What fortune is worth losing your soul over? What things can bring you peace of mind? Remember, you *must* leave it all behind when you die. Don't be captured by idolatry.

## Immorality

Immorality was a major stumbling block to the children of Israel. Sounds like today, doesn't it? I know it does, because young men often come to me, crying things like, "Pastor Tom, I'm so sorry I fell into immorality for the ninth time this week." I respond: "Brother, you didn't fall into anything. You jumped in with both feet."

What such "victims" need is the fear of God. It will restrain them from committing evil. Fear—meaning love, reverence, and respect for Him—will cause you to hate sin and stop the sinful behavior. This is the secret of practicing Christians. They aren't "goodie two shoes" who are afraid to do something wrong. They wisely recognize they can be tempted and need God's restraint.

These men who wail about their sin are really expressing the displeasure caused by guilt. It reminds me of my childhood when I gulped down a dozen chocolate chip cookies. Mom warned me not to touch the next batch because they were for guests. Breaking "the law" meant Dad's 36-inch alligator skin belt would land on my rear end. Guess what? The fear of punishment only lasted through the third cookie. Dad suddenly appeared. Evidence crumbled from the corners of my mouth. Seeing him reach for his belt, I screamed, "No, Daddy, no Daddy, I'm sorry, I'm sorry!" He glared: "Son, you're not really sorry. You're just sorry you got caught." Deservedly, I suffered the consequences of my disobedience.

In much the same way, the Bible describes the two types of repentance. Second Corinthians 7:9–10 says, "I now rejoice, not that you were made sorrowful, but that you were made sorrowful to the point of repentance; for you were made sorrowful according to the will of God, in order that you might not suffer loss in anything through us. For the sorrow that is according to the will of God produces a repentance without regret, leading to salvation; but the sorrow of the world produces death."

Repentance means turning around and going the other way. It is like the about-face you make if you mistakenly enter a one-way street. It is the type of repentance needed to solve our society's moral crisis. Young men in America hear dozens of voices telling them to throw away their virtue and run after all kinds of unholy practices. Sexually-transmitted diseases are running wild. Teen pregnancy is skyrocketing. Our generation is addicted to pornography and masturbation. Homosexual advocates teach their sin as a normal, alternate lifestyle. Advertisers use sex to sell everything from beer to fountain pens.

Is it any wonder we have problems when rock stars like Madonna brag that losing her virginity was a career move? This from a woman who was voted the top idol of teenage girls in the 1980s. At the beginning of the decade, *Glamour* magazine named her one of the ten most influential women in America. Even though her popularity seems to be fading now, her past influence lives on—and don't worry, somebody else will take her place. Such distorted moral stands mislead young women, who think this is the way to fame and popularity. And so with hot young men, who mistakenly believe that most women feel that way.

In addition, erroneous evolutionary teachers tell us man is just another rung on the animal ladder. They say we should act out our animalistic desires. Sir Julian Huxley, the first head of the biology department at Rice University, was once asked in a British television interview why evolution was so readily accepted by the scientific community. His candid reply: "I suppose the reason we jumped at *The Origin of the Species* was because the idea of God interfered with our sexual mores."[3] Commenting on the outrage the remark stirred in the scientific community, famed minister and author D. James Kennedy noted the scientists didn't deny the truth of the statement. "But they didn't want to tell the whole world that their acceptance of absurd notions was actually motivated by their lust and their rejection of God."[4]

Many of Huxley's contemporaries describe sex as a biological urge. That is true with animals. Not humans. God created us to be moral, rational, reasoning human beings with the capacity to obey moral laws and hold to a code of ethics. Jesus set the rules in Matthew 5:28: every man who looks lustfully on a woman has committed adultery in his heart.

The Lord gives this extreme remedy in verses 29–30, "And if your right eye makes you stumble, tear it out, and throw it from you; for it is better for you that one of the parts of your body perish, than for your whole body to be thrown into hell. And if your right hand makes you stumble, cut it off, and throw it from you."

Thank goodness Jesus didn't mean that literally! Otherwise, we would all be walking around with a patch over one eye and two stumps for arms. The point Jesus was making is, we must ruthlessly fight lust and other sin. Wimpy, mediocre men don't want to stop their wrongdoing. They want to compromise or justify their weakness. God gives no room for excuses, saying, *"Cut it off."*

You are not alone in your struggle against pornography, homosexuality, or fornication (sex outside of marriage). But if you are to ever have any hope of overcoming these sins, you must first agree with God that these things are wrong. Otherwise, there is no reason to change. Pray daily for power over the temptation to lust. Then have faith that God's grace will give you the ability to overcome.

Remember, lust is a master passion. Either you master the passion or it masters you. Are you involved in a romantic relationship? God wants that relationship to be holy and pure. Do you really love a girl? If so, you will keep your hands off and your pants on until you're married. This proves your love and will build respect and trust. I learned the following definitions of lust and love from Ed Cole during my travels with him. Judge your relationship by them.

- Lust always takes at the *expense of others* for the gratification of *self*. Lust is never satisfied. Though it craves intimacy, lust is a counterfeit of what only prayer can produce. It leaves you lacking fulfillment, security, and lasting satisfaction. Lust enslaves you. Spirits that hate you overtake you and addict you to unhealthy desires. Lust leads you down a path of increasingly repulsive sin. At the end of the road, you're tormented by the consequences of your immorality.

- Love always gives at the *expense of self* for the gratification of *others*. The Bible says love is easily satisfied. Remember, Jesus faced all kinds of temptations, just like you and me. But not once did He fall into sin. He was intimate with His Heavenly Father, providing Him a deep sense of sovereignty and power. Godly love will produce those same qualities in you.

## Trying the Lord

The third deadly sin that will keep you from the "promised land" is trying the Lord. This means asking God to do something out of His character, contrary to His will. For example, asking for His blessings in school, yet failing to study and making up for it by cheating. Or business owners who pray for God's favor but "fudge" on their income tax. That is trying the Lord.

Another variation of this sin is the old line, "God, I'll serve You if _____." You can fill in the blank with statements like, "If you let me marry Susie," or "If you let me make the varsity football team," or "If you get me that good job." But God isn't the host of "Let's Make a Deal." We don't pick Christianity door number 1, 2, or 3. Jesus would say, "Let's Make a Deal?' No thanks. I'd rather play 'Truth or Consequences.'"

Yet, millions treat Christianity like a huge cafeteria line. They think serving God is like a buffet: "Oh, fellowship? Yeah, give me a plate of that. Answered prayer? Pile it on. That green stuff called prosperity? Right, I can handle a bunch of that. Holiness? Uh . . . no thanks, had some last month. Kinda hard to digest." We can't come to God on such terms. He says, "Hey, friend, where I lead, you'll follow. What I feed, you'll swallow."

That is why it turns my stomach to see the charm around some people's necks: *Try God.* What a mistaken notion! You don't "try" God like you would broccoli, asparagus, or liver. You might as well tell Satan, "Hey, just make the going tough enough or long enough and I'll quit." When you are born again, you enter into a marriage with the Lord, a relationship sealed by a decision of your will.

Imagine it's your wedding day. The pastor asks, "Do you take this woman to be your lawfully wedded wife, to love, honor, and cherish her all the days of your life?" What do you think would happen if you answered, "I'll try"? She might drop you like a bad habit! Or she might scream, "Try this size seven shoe over your head!" Your loved one wants commitment. So does Jesus.

"Oh, but that's so hard," men often whine. "I'm not perfect. I have normal urges." I met such a man once. A hulking football player at USC, he told me he was about 75 to 80 percent committed to Jesus. "That's not good enough," I said. "That won't get you anywhere but hell."

"I'm trying, Tom, but nobody's perfect."

"Oh really?" I asked. "How committed to playing football are you?" He glared back and said proudly, "One hundred and ten percent." I pressed him, asking: "What makes that so? Is it because you never blew any assignments? Never missed any tackles? Never lost a game?"

Waving his hand in the air, he whimpered: "No, Tom, you don't understand. It's my heart, my desire. I'm giving it my all." I responded, "Now you understand. That's what Jesus wants from you. All of your heart!"

It's not that Christians never make mistakes. Everyone falls short. If we didn't, we wouldn't need Jesus. But God looks at our sincerity. Once you make a decision to serve God and put your will in agreement with His, you can live a life that pleases Him. God will release an abundance of grace to give you the ability.

It's like the three Hebrew men in the Book of Daniel, Shadrach, Meshach, and Abednego. The king demanded they bow down and worship his false god or he would throw them into a fiery furnace (so hot it killed the men who hauled them to the furnace door—now that's smokin'!). Yet, these young men had decided they weren't going to bow down, even if it cost them their lives.

They could have wimped out and found an excuse, like timid believers in a restaurant. I've seen them praying their "headache prayers." They rub their forehead and quickly mumble a few words, hoping no one notices them. Or worse, says nothing. But these three courageous men experienced the power of a right decision. God delivered them. They weren't just *trying* to serve God. They *did*. And so can you!

## Craving Evil

The fourth sin that will keep you out of the "promised land" is found in 1 Corinthians 10:6: "That we should not crave evil things, as they also craved." Israel experienced miraculous deliverance from Egypt. Yet, they still weren't satisfied. When things didn't run smoothly, they groaned (I'm paraphrasing), "Oh, Moses, if we were only back in Egypt. We had bread and meat to eat there. Now we're in this crummy wilderness. We don't have water, it's too hot, and we'll die. Oh, if we could only return to Egypt."

What an attitude! They cried out in Egypt because of the cruelty of their slavemasters. As soon as they escaped that misery they forgot about it and started griping that things were too hard. Moses deserved their gratitude, not their grumbling.

But how different is that from casual Christians who come to God today based on what they can get from Him? Those looking for ease of living, no sacrifice, no commitment, and no wilderness experiences. At the first sign of trouble, they are quick to complain: "Oh, this is too hard. Why is God giving me all these problems?"

Many evangelists cater to them, preaching "easy believism." Their altar calls sound like this: "Friends, if you want your sins forgiven, if you want eternal life, if you have needs, if you have been scarred by rejection and need healing in your heart, if you want acceptance with the Lord, then come to the altar as we pray."

Thank God that Jesus gives us forgiveness and eternal life. Who doesn't want healing, understanding, and salvation? But don't forget the commitment. Matthew 10:38 says, "And he who does not take his cross and follow after Me is not worthy of Me." You've often heard the term *selling out*, probably in negative terms. Think of it in a positive way when it comes to Christ. We must sell out our desires for Him. Otherwise, we will be counterfeit converts who crave evil and yield to lustful passions.

Many claim to be born again without the evidence of genuine Christian fruit. They may look like disciples of Jesus and talk as though they know the Lord. Yet, they have not been converted. Their commitment is incomplete. Inside their hearts, they are holding on to the world, symbolized in the Bible by Egypt.

They appear genuine. Yet, inside they crave evil. Dig through their wallets and there are packs of condoms. Check their music collections and you will see lots of heavy metal but no Christian tunes. Check their personal habits and you will discover they can watch three hours of TV or videos per day, but can never find time to read the Bible.

The sin of craving evil will keep you locked into old habits. It reminds me of the old story about the man who tried to change his pet pig into a dog. Ever since it was a piglet, he trained it. He fed the pig Alpo, gave him a bright gold collar and cleaned him with a scrub brush. When it came time to take his trained "dog" for a walk, they had gone only a block before the pig saw a mud puddle. Breaking his leash and shaking off his gold collar, he raced for the puddle to enjoy a mud bath. He had experienced a dog's life, but he was still a pig. *His nature had not changed.* Remember, man can change a habit, but only God can change a nature.

Counterfeit converts are the same. Unless Jesus Christ, by the power of the Holy Spirit, changes sinners' hearts they will jump back into the mud puddle of sin. Ed Cole once told me: "Take a man with sin in his life and educate him and you have an educated sinner. Take him to a psychiatrist and you create an adjusted sinner. Put him in rehabilitation to produce a rehabilitated sinner. Sit him in the front pew at church and, without the Holy Spirit's power, all you'll see is a religious sinner." Does your heart still crave evil? Do you practice sins the Bible condemns? Then you are not a disciple of Christ, but a counterfeit convert.

It insults God when you claim that you are one of His children on Sunday and live for the devil the other six days a week. Search your heart to see if there is any hidden sin, or areas of life you have not surrendered to God. Pray about it and the Holy Spirit will bring them to mind. You can't crave evil and enjoy a relationship with our holy Heavenly Father.

## Grumbling

The Bible says in Hebrews 11:6 that without faith it is impossible to please God. Grumbling is the exact opposite of faithfulness. When the children of Israel griped against God, they showed they did not trust Him to meet their needs. What's worse, a grumbling spirit causes you to become cynical. . . the kind of person who, when someone says, "Have a nice day," sneers, "I have other plans." Grumbling has other symptoms:

- Fault-finding
- Spreading rumors, which causes strife and disunity
- Complaining
- Ungratefulness
- Unforgiveness

- Continuous negative speech

- Undermining authority

A grumbling spirit reveals whether you serve God out of love or compulsion. It reveals whether you serve God with joy or out of a sense of duty, meaning you feel you have to do it to get to heaven. Grumblers see only difficult duties and no delights in taking God's message to the world. What's worse, speaking negatively provokes negative feelings in others. It drives you (and them) deeper into doubt and unbelief. There you become easy prey for the devil.

Jude 12–13 calls grumblers, "Hidden reefs [or stains] in your love feasts when they feast with you without fear, caring for themselves; clouds without water, carried along by winds; autumn trees without fruit, doubly dead, uprooted; wild waves of the sea, casting up their own shame like foam; wandering stars, for whom the black darkness has been reserved forever." Verse 16 adds, "These are grumblers, finding fault, following after their own lusts."

When you feel a grumbling spirit or negative words coming out of your mouth, combat it in two ways:

1. Develop a spirit of thankfulness for all the Lord has done for you. Concentrate on all the wonderful things He's done in your life.

2. In difficult situations, write down, and then speak, what the Word of God says about them. If your teacher or boss hands you a seemingly impossible assignment, say things like: "All things are possible to him who believes" (Mark 9:23), "My grace is sufficient for you" (2 Cor. 12:9), "I can do all things through Him who strengthens me" (Phil. 4:13), or "The joy of the Lord is your [my] strength" (Neh. 8:10).

Resist grumbling, even though thankfulness might be the last thing on your mind, even if you're so upset you don't want to consider praising God. As you do this, it won't be long before God's peace and grace overtakes you.

That is why it's so important to read God's Word, the Bible. In discipling men, I set a goal of one hour per day in Bible reading and prayer. It's not an absolute must, but this standard proves personally rewarding. It doesn't always happen right away. Sometimes men will make it thirty minutes, then gradually move up to forty, fifty and then sixty minutes.

Occasionally, some accuse me of legalism. Generally, the root of their problem is acknowledging Jesus as Lord of their lives. If someone doesn't want to spend time with Jesus, I question whether they are committed to Him. Spiritually malnourished and insensitive to God's will, such a person wanders through life's wilderness, always blaming God for his problems. If you will get into God's Word and spend time talking with Him in prayer, you will discover it's a sure-fire cure for grumbling.

## Conclusion

These five stumbling blocks kept the children of Israel from their divine destiny. They are the same five traps the devil baits for your destruction. When I talk about being free of idolatry, immorality, trying the Lord, craving evil, and grumbling, I'm not talking about fanatical faith. This is the fruit of every disciple of Christ.

Living holy and pure should be "baby food" to the Christian. But working to put aside these five deadly sins in your personal life will bring a promotion to greater purposes. You will advance the kingdom of God and become a leader in this generation. Don't fall into these five fatal traps. Don't sell out to momentary ease, comfort, and pleasure in this life, only to forfeit eternity. You may feel like you're wandering around in the wilderness right now, but you're not alone. God brought you out of slavery to sin. Don't go back to it.

If you need to ask Jesus into your heart for the first time, and have your nature changed from a sinner to a child of God—or if you are caught up in one of the five sins listed in this chapter—I want to offer you the chance to pray a prayer of repentance and ask Jesus to forgive you. He will give you the power to live as a Christian should live. Say it aloud:

"Lord Jesus, I want to stop trusting in myself and in what I can do. I want to start trusting in You and what You did for me when You died for me on the cross. I know that I am a sinner and I am sorry for my sins. I ask You to forgive me. I invite You to come and live inside of me. I want You to be my Savior and my Lord, which means being first in every area of my life. I want to repent and turn away from everything that You and the Bible call sin. I totally commit myself to obeying You every day, for the rest of my life. Thank You, Jesus, for forgiving me and washing away my sins so that I can be a new creation in You."

Now that you have committed your life to Him, read on to learn how you can attain the spirit of might needed to achieve greatness for Jesus' glory.

### Gut Check

1. From the list of five reasons you won't enter your promised land, which areas are your worst weakness? Write down your problems or explain them to a small group of close friends.

a. Idols (what you think about or crave).

b. Immorality (lust).

c. Trying God (demanding that He do something contrary to His nature or character).

d. Craving evil in your heart.

e. Grumbling (complaining, fault finding, unforgiveness).

2. What safeguards have you set up to strengthen your defenses against such sins? List them. For example, if you struggle with lust, make a decision to clean your mind daily with God's Word. On the practical side, decide not to go behind "closed doors" or be alone with a woman. Note: if you are struggling for answers, ask your pastor, discipler, or other mature Christian for ideas.

3. Have you accepted Jesus as your Savior? What are you going to do about it?

4. From your heart, write out your personal pledge of allegiance to Jesus Christ.

# 5

## THE SPIRIT OF MIGHT

*God, give us mighty men. The time demands*
*Strong minds, great hearts,*
*True faith and willing hands;*
*Men whom the lust of office does not kill;*
*Men whom the spoils of office cannot buy;*
*Men who possess opinions and a will;*
*Men who have honor, men who will not lie;*
*Men who can stand before a demagogue*
*And damn his treacherous flatteries without winking;*
*Tall men, sun-crowned men, who live above the fog*
*In public duty and in private thinking.*

*—Poet John G. Holland*[1]

I N CHAPTER 2, I MENTIONED HOW A. C. GREEN challenges others to answer the call. This Phoenix Suns' star is a shining example of a man with the spirit of might. When a reporter asked him how he reconciled his religious beliefs with playing a rough game, he replied: "God wants His people to be warriors, battlers and fighters. And I don't mean waging warfare, or getting into fights. What I mean is being a battler and fighter in doing as well as you can in your chosen occupation. I don't think any Christian should be a passive kind of person. If he is, then he's going to be headed for a lot of problems in his spiritual walk . . . Just look at God's warriors in the Bible. They were always ready to fight, destroy their enemies and possess their land. It's that spirit of might that moves me. I don't start anything but I won't back down either."[2]

The might I'm talking about is not inherited; it's given to us by Jesus Christ. Second Corinthians 13:4 gives an example: "For indeed He [Christ] was crucified because of weakness, yet He lives because of the *power of God*. For we also are weak in Him, yet we shall live with Him because of the *power of God* directed toward you" (italics added). First Corinthians 1:26–27 says, "For consider your calling, brethren, that there were not many wise according to the flesh, *not many mighty*, not many noble; but God has chosen the foolish things of the world to shame the wise, and God has chosen the weak things of the world to shame the things which are strong" (italics added).

In the original Hebrew, "might" is defined as "the inherent power to do anything." According to Ephesians 3:16, that power is available to us through our Heavenly Father: "That He would grant you, according to the riches of His glory, to be strengthened with power [might] through His Spirit in the inner man" [our spirit man]. Read on in Ephesians and you'll see that the purpose of this might is so we can be rooted and grounded in Christ.

## Commitment

Many Christians are not firmly rooted, committed to standing their ground. Without a strong source of faith, they fade in the face of pressure. The parable of the seed and the sower in Mark 4:16–17 gives an example of people with great joy. But, because they have "no firm root in themselves, but are only temporary; then, when affliction or persecution arises because of the word, immediately they fall away."

Why is it so important to get rooted in faith through Jesus Christ? So we can put an end to TCS: Temporary Christian Syndrome. God wants to make you mighty in this generation, one that has major problems. If you're in your late teens or early twenties, you may have been one of the respondents to a survey that the Young Life ministry did a few years ago of church youngsters thirteen to eighteen. They discovered that the average teen member answers altar calls during revivals, crusades, and other events sixteen times. That's about three times a year!

I wondered, *What's wrong with our altar calls?* After all, when the average American teenage Christian asks Jesus into his heart sixteen times, something is lacking. But it's not the altar calls. It's the way those young people are left dangling after they repent and pray to make Christ Lord over their life. Follow-up and discipleship are missing many times.

For a commitment that lasts, young men need a "spirit of might." As Paul writes in 2 Corinthians 13:3, that Christ "is not weak toward you, but *mighty in you*" (italics added). Job 22:8 adds, "The earth belongs to the mighty man." This spirit of might helps a man avoid compromising his morals, rise above fear, and stand against wickedness. The indomitable spirit that only God can give will keep you, in the midst of trials and temptations, from turning "belly up" and quitting.

## Slow and Clumsy

You might think: *Well, what can I do? I'm pretty weak and clumsy. I could never stand out in a crowd. People would ignore me if I tried to lead them anywhere.* Brother, I know just what you're thinking because that's exactly the way I once felt. As a fat, uncoordinated boy of eight, I craved acceptance and friendship. I failed second grade because I couldn't go around the rings in the school yard. My parents took me to a nearby university for testing to find out why I had a "learning disability." That increased my insecurity. I thought: *There must be something wrong with me. I'm not normal like other kids.*

Even though the tests showed I had above-average intelligence, the damage was done. As I shared in chapter 1, I struggled for identity and acceptance through athletics and girlfriends, only to find they were masks for my insecurity. It took Jesus to get me out of the cave. I want to encourage others in similar situations. There is hope! Your life is *not* worthless. You have *value.* Jesus wants to give you a glorious purpose.

Remember, God is the master of turning the weak into the strong. He molds wimps into warriors, chumps into champs, and mama's boys into military men. As Ed Cole says, "Champions are not those who never fail, they are those who *never quit!*" My prayer is that God will mold you into a true champion for Christ.

## Mighty Men

One of my favorite Bible stories is about a group of mighty men: namely, David and his four hundred supporters. First Chronicles 11:10–23 lists some of their feats. They fought lions, broke behind enemy lines, and wiped out three hundred of the opposition at one time. Chapter 12 lists some of their characteristics. They have the qualities that will provide the battle plan for a consistent, victorious Christian walk. (Before reading further, I encourage you to stop and look at these two chapters.)

When I first read about them, I thought, *Wow, what a bunch of studs!* I imagined hulks with 21-inch biceps. Bursting with supernatural courage and relentless determination. Trained from birth to be champions and heroes. An example of society's "cream of the crop." However, 1 Samuel 22:1–2 paints an entirely different portrait. When David fled from King Saul in Israel, to the cave of Adullam, guess who followed? "Everyone who was in distress, and everyone who was in debt, and everyone who was discontented, gathered to him; and he became captain over them. Now there were about four hundred men with him."

In other words, they were hopeless, broke, and bitter; homeless rejects that modern society would label misfits or troublemakers. Can you imagine what David thought when he saw this ragtag bunch approaching? Something like: *Oh, great, just what I need. I'm shut up in a cave, Saul is after my head and now this? God, why have You forsaken me?*

For a minute, forget about David's ancient cave. There are many young men right now who identify with David's men. They have been branded worthless, and are stuck in despair and hopelessness. Their caves are peer rejection, depression, anxiety, or addiction to alcohol, drugs, and immorality. Mired in dens of insecurity, their failure pulls them into further despair.

Maybe that's how you feel today. Well, don't despair. Read on to learn more about David's mighty men. These heroes had five qualities, the same ones that will make you strong and help you stand in the midst of wickedness. They were: (1) not men-pleasers, (2) trained and equipped, (3) bold, (4) quick to obey the Lord, and, (5) had understanding and purpose.

In today's society, Christians are the new villains. Our beliefs are distorted by the news media, entertainers, and educators. Gay rights activists, feminists, pro-abortionists, and some political leaders frequently label all Christians as narrow-minded fundamentalists.

Prayer has been outlawed from our public schools, Bible studies often are silenced on campus, and students face discipline for sharing about their faith. Groups like the American Civil Liberties Union are on the prowl against all public displays of Christianity, even though faith played an integral part in America's founding. At my alma mater (USC), a small band of anti-Christian activists removed these horrible words from our diplomas, "In the Year of Our Lord."

*Washington Post* political cartoonist Patrick Oliphant once pictured Christians as rats dragging the Republican elephant into a mission, with a "Jesus Saves" sign above the door. When Christians called the Capitol to protest President Clinton's lifting of the ban on homosexuals in the military, the *Post* carried a horrible article referring to Christians as "poor, uneducated and easy to command."[3] A public outcry forced the *Post* to make a retraction after this outrageous article appeared. Yet, it's hard to imagine an ethnic minority group treated so shabbily without any major repercussions.

These are just a few instances of how unpopular it is to be a Christian in this generation. In many social arenas, faith is viewed as politically incorrect. But if you want to serve Jesus, politically correct thinking will never replace righteous beliefs. The mighty man is consumed with looking good in God's sight, not man's.

Where can we find the inspiration to become the mighty men needed for this age? First Chronicles 12 reveals how the band of debtors, losers, and misfits who came to David turned into such great warriors. In applying their qualities, we can ensure long-lasting success in our walk with God and in our life among fellow human beings. As Joel 3:10 declares, "Let the weak say, 'I am a mighty man.'"

David's followers faced tough choices. Because they picked God's way instead of man's, they enjoyed great success. Realize that God first tested them because He wanted to establish His kingdom with them. David ruled through these tried, tested, and loyal men. Their preparation and commitment made them disproportionately powerful. As God did for David's men, He will surely do for you.

### Please, No Men-Pleasers

First Chronicles 12:1–2 says, "Now these are the ones who came to David at Ziklag, while he was still restricted because of Saul the son of Kish; and they were among the mighty men who helped him in war. They were equipped with bows, using both the right hand and the left to sling stones and to shoot arrows from the bow; they were Saul's kinsmen from Benjamin."

This passage lists the first quality it takes to make you mighty: avoid being a man-pleaser. First and foremost, David's men were loyal. Verse 2 says some of them came from the family of King Saul, David's bitter enemy. But they were willing to be disowned rather than be out of God's will. They would lay down their lives for David, even though he wasn't in the ruling party. A man-pleaser is more concerned about what friends, peers, family, or business partners believe about a given situation than what God's Word says.

To better understand this concept, look at Pontius Pilate, the Bible's king of the man-pleasers. Tormented all night by a dream about Jesus, his wife warned Pilate to have nothing to do with Him. Even the ruler testified that he couldn't find any fault with Jesus. But when the crowd cried out, "If you release this Man, you are no friend of Caesar" (John 19:12), Pilate caved in to his fear of man and allowed Jesus to be crucified.

Like David's men, modern fighters must avoid "Pilate" consciousness. Just as in ancient Roman days, it is not popular to call yourself a Christian. As I mentioned earlier, a Christian label attracts all kinds of opposition. Among other things, you are likely to be branded "a phony hypocrite" or someone "trying to force morality down our throats." The spirit of man-pleasing controls today's young generation. It causes them to bow down to peer pressure. It takes a God-given spirit of might to stand against these forces and dare to hold onto Christian convictions, morals, and values.

Fearing confrontation or ridicule, a man-pleaser is afraid to confess his allegiance to Jesus Christ. Examples include the athlete who stands silent in the locker room while dirty jokes fly, the businessman who won't speak against profanity for fear of losing a deal, or the fraternity brother who drinks with the crowd for the sake of acceptance.

Ever do any of those things? Consider Jesus' words in Matthew 10:32–33: "Everyone therefore who shall confess Me before men, I will also confess him before My Father who is in heaven. But whoever shall deny Me before men, I will also deny him before My Father who is in heaven."

Now, who do you want to please: men or God?

## Trained and Equipped

The second quality needed for might in this generation comes from 1 Chronicles 12:12: "They were equipped with bows, using both the right hand and the left to sling stones and to shoot arrows from the bow." The key phrase is: *they were equipped.*

Most struggling believers don't fail on the basis of desire. They just haven't been trained. They don't know about prayer, daily Bible reading, or the art of spiritual warfare. Christians are to be soldiers in God's army, able to handle the sword of the spirit (God's Word). Too many soldiers are AWOL (absent without leave), coasting along without any kind of discipleship. Discipleship means training, which comes from two sources: the church and the Word of God.

The church plays a vital role in a Christian's life. It is often referred to as the body of Christ, with Jesus as the head. First Corinthians 12:18 says, "But now God has placed the members, each one of them, *in the body,* just as He desired" (italics added). Ephesians 2:19 calls us "fellow citizens with the saints," while 1 Peter 2:5 says we are "living stones" built into God's house.

The church's two-fold purpose is for your protection (giving you a spiritual covering) and for your perfection (building you up in the faith). If you expect to grow in your relationship with God, you must be committed to a body of believers where the Bible is taught. (See Eph. 4:11–14.) There are too many independent "Lone Rangers" wandering without spiritual leadership. God wants you serving Him from a proper position in His house.

The church also fulfills what is known as the "five-fold ministry." Ephesians 4:11 lists them: apostle, prophet, evangelist, pastor, and teacher. According to the Bible, these ministries build up the body of Christ in unity of faith and maturity. This training causes people to grow up and act more like Christ.

The church's primary function is summed up in Ephesians 4:12: "for the *equipping* of the saints for the work of service," with the outcome, "the building up of the body of Christ." Note it does not say, "for the entertaining of the saints," or "the baby-sitting of the saints," or even, "the hospitalization of the saints." God wants you to be an integral part of His body, the church, so you can be trained to establish His ways on the earth. God wants healthy, mature, and strong Christians, but apart from His church there will be no other means of attaining this goal.

Likewise, you will draw strength from God's Word. Second Timothy 3:16–17 says, "All Scripture is inspired by God and profitable for teaching, for reproof, for correction, for training in righteousness, that the man of God may be adequate, equipped for every good work." In other words, *every time* you sit down with the Bible, it's teaching, reproving, correcting, and training you.

I once read a shocking statistic in the Gallup Poll. While an overwhelming majority of Americans professed to be born again, less than 10 percent read their Bibles daily. Compare this with Jesus' statements in John 14:15, 23–24, "If you love Me, you will keep My commandments. . . . If anyone loves Me, he will keep My word; and My Father will love him, and We will come to him, and make Our abode with him. He who does not love Me does not keep My words."

The supreme test of your love for God is whether you are keeping His Word! The small numbers who love it enough to read it every day show our generation's three greatest sins: indifference to, neglect of, and disrespect for God's Word. Daily reading and study is a must. If you can't take an hour, start with 20 minutes. Remember that success starts with desire. It takes 30 days to develop a habit. From desire to discipline to delight. If you set aside the next four weeks to meet Jesus daily in His holy Word, it will revolutionize your life. Few have the courage to live this way. Real men do.

### Boldness

First Chronicles 12:8 lists the next two qualities of a mighty man, starting with an extraordinary spirit of boldness. It reads, "And from the Gadites there came over to David in the stronghold in the wilderness, mighty men of valor, men trained for war, who could handle shield and spear, and whose faces were like the faces of lions, and they were as swift as the gazelles on the mountains."

These men are described as looking like lions. In the Bible, lions represent boldness. As Proverbs 28:1 says, "The righteous are bold as a lion." This quality is a supernatural confidence in the midst of conflict and confrontation. The lion would rather die than be outfought. Is this your attitude? Would you rather die than deny the name of Jesus or compromise your convictions?

We don't see many bold Christians today because not many are walking in righteousness, or right standing, with God. If you want to be bold, get sin out of your life. It's hard to be bold if you're wondering if someone will expose your "Saturday-night-parties, Sunday-morning-church" habit. A clean conscience makes for easy boldness.

As a young man I always followed the crowd. Though a tough football player, insecurity dominated my inner feelings. In speech class, for example, I trembled when my turn came. However, after I repented of my sin, I joined a dynamic campus ministry. They stressed that you had to be bold to be a Christian. I knew it would only be a matter of time before I had to make my stand, too.

During my senior year I signed up for a marketing class. The young professor wanted to "relate" to his students. So the first day he announced, "Let's have some fun and get to know each other. Why don't we go around the room and share our erotic fantasies?" I broke into a cold sweat, thinking, *Oh, no, I'm going to have to be bold. That's what they've been telling me. But since I'm in the last seat on the last row, maybe he won't call on me.*

No such luck. After a dozen stories, the instructor said, "Mr. Sirotnak? Why don't you share your fantasies?" Though I was scared, I had made up my mind that I would speak up. The Holy Spirit gave me the right words. Boldness rose up inside, and I said, "Sir, up to now I've had many erotic fantasies. But I've been born again, and all I have now are supernatural realities; and I would be glad to tell you about those! I want to see the whole world filled with the glory of God. I want to see the life-changing news of Jesus Christ preached to every student on campus. But above all else, I want to see perverted professors delivered from their erotic fantasies."

The class grew stone silent. The professor's only response was, stammering "I will never call on you again." I got an A in that class. More importantly, Jesus was glorified. You may be thinking, *I can't do that.* Yes, you can! I grew into boldness gradually. It didn't come overnight. There were other times when I missed opportunities to take a stand. Instead of feeling guilty, I used them to provoke me the next time. Boldness is not just volume of voice. It's the willingness to speak. You will never make an impact without a collision.

We need bold men who will dare to influence their generation. But even more important we need brave young men on our high school and college campuses who will unashamedly serve as lights in the midst of darkness. Andrew Jackson, the seventh president of the United States, once said, "One man with courage makes a majority."[4] Will you dare to be that one?

## Quick Obedience

First Chronicles 12:8 says, "They were as swift as the gazelles on the mountains." That doesn't mean David's men just ran fast or took swift action. It symbolizes their quick obedience to God. We, too, must obey the Lord without hesitation. Obedience displays a passion to please God and drives us to pursue holiness. It's like Moses telling Israel (Deut. 23:14), "Since the Lord your God walks in the midst of your camp to deliver you and to defeat your enemies before you, therefore your camp must be holy; and He must not see anything indecent among you lest He turn away from you."

Likewise, we must put indecent things away from our lives. The off-color soap operas, pornographic videos, filthy rap music, swearing, boozing it up . . . the list of junk the world considers "normal" could fill this book. We must not be presumptuous and defiant of God's law, without any fear of Him. We cannot justify our sin and expect Him to ignore it. God commands us to be holy. First Peter 1:13–16 says, "Therefore, gird your minds for action, keep sober in spirit, fix your hope completely on the grace to be brought to you at the revelation of Jesus Christ. *As obedient children,* do not be conformed to the former lusts which were yours in your ignorance, but like the Holy One who called you, be holy yourselves also in all your behavior; because it is written, 'You shall be holy, for I am holy'" (italics added).

If God commanded us to be holy, then He will also give us the grace and power to do it. Right now, if God is convicting you of uncleanness in your life, repent and ask Him to give you the grace to depart forever from it.

### Understanding and Purpose

The fifth characteristic of David's mighty men is found in 1 Chronicles 12:32, "And of the sons of Issachar, men who understood the times, with knowledge of what Israel should do." They were men who realized they had a part in God's overall plan and created change in their society.

The Republicans may understand the times and the Democrats may understand the times, but very few know what to do. Men of knowledge and wisdom will never replace men of understanding and purpose. Knowledge is simply acquiring facts. Wisdom is interpreting them. But understanding is applying them. That's why our crying need is for educated men who will apply godly answers to the problems facing our world.

We need solution bearers for this lost society. We must have strong, mighty Christian men in every sphere of society, whether in business, law, medicine, politics, the arts, sports, the media, or science. Christian men, full of God's understanding, applying wisdom and truth across this land, will boost us out of moral decay.

### Conclusion

The goal of Christian training is to impact our nation and world with Christ's gospel. Are you prepared to take your key position? God wants to exalt you, but will you be ready? We can't be Christian airheads, singing "Kumbaya, Lord" at weenie roasts, while the world is going down the tubes. We must know the problems from a Biblical perspective and reason out solutions.

Don't wait for the rapture to take you out of this dirty world. Put your hands in the dirt and trust God to create something awesome. Namely, His kingdom on earth as it is in heaven. Maybe you can't do it all. But you can do your part. To take this step, you will need strong principles. So read on to chapter 6 to learn the difference between conviction and preference.

## Gut Check

1. Write down your definition of a mighty man. Is it more important how you look and are accepted in public or who you are and what you believe?

2. Are you a member of a local church where the Bible is actively taught and practiced? If not, prayerfully ask the Lord where you should go to become a useful part of God's family.

3. Do you have a discipler or a man to whom you are accountable for your actions? If not, make an appointment with your pastor or spiritual leader and tell him about your desire for spiritual growth and accountability. We all need a spiritual "coach" who can objectively and lovingly bring us into the maturity of a man of God.

4. What other training will further your relationship and calling with Jesus Christ (such as books, seminars, conventions, Bible studies, etc.)? List a plan for getting more training.

5. Is it possible to reverse America's moral decay? If so, what is your part?

# 6

## PUT UP OR SHUT UP

*He who believes is strong, he who doubts is weak. Strong convictions precede great actions.*

—*Anonymous*

L EGENDARY WORLD WAR II HERO General George S. Patton Jr. trained his troops to hate the Nazis. In a series of speeches to the Third Army on May 31, 1944, he said, "I actually pity those poor ———— we're going up against. I do. We're not just going to shoot the ————, we're going to cut out their living guts and use them to grease the treads of our tanks. We're going to murder those lousy Hun ———— by the bushel. Now some of you boys, I know, are wondering whether or not you'll chicken out under fire. Don't worry about it. I can assure you that you'll all do your duty. The Nazis are the enemy. Wade into them. Spill their blood, shoot them in the belly. When you put your hand into a bunch of goo that a moment before was your best friend's face, you'll know what to do."[1]

Pardon the rough language, but it makes a point. Patton taught his men to hate because, if they hated the enemy, they would fight fearlessly. How I wish the Christian men of our generation would develop this kind of attitude. Not for people, but about sin and ungodly injustice. We would revolutionize the world in a decade. Not by hating others, but by hating the devil and all his works.

Convictions build a hatred for sin. You don't want to touch it or have anything to do with it. Psalm 97:10 warns, "Hate evil, you who love the Lord, Who preserves the souls of His godly ones." Proverbs 8:13 adds, "The fear of the Lord is to hate evil; Pride and arrogance and the evil way, and the perverted mouth, I hate." If you develop convictions, your hatred of evil will permit you to resist and overcome it.

Remember this statement: "What you tolerate you cannot change." It is easy to get worked up over our culture's sin. Pro-abortion, pro-homosexual, and anti-Christian philosophies dominate our media and public education. But what about your pet sins? Personal compromises like premarital sex, telling "white" lies to make yourself look good, copying movies rented from the video store, using computer software without paying for it, or listening to filthy music . . . the things you do quietly, and then cover up and justify.

Now, I am a man just like you, not some super Christian. There are areas where I am are more susceptible to stumbling into sin. However, the nearer I draw to God, the more I see that my hatred for sin is directly proportional to my love for God. As I spend time daily with Jesus in His Word, convictions are formulated and He changes me, little by little, into His image.

Tennis star Andre Agassi does a commercial for Canon cameras where he boasts, "Image is everything." That's true. But not self-image or vain, shallow, exterior appearances. Godly image is everything. Man is to reflect the image and glory of God (1 Cor. 11:7). That takes convictions. As I began to grasp this truth, I started viewing the world's system—with its indoctrination in sinful lusts—through the eyes of my Father. This produced a greater distaste for ungodly practices, especially those in my own life. As you walk closer with God, you too will develop a resistance that opposes the works of sin.

One example of a man whose convictions guide his decisions is legendary pro football great Bubba Smith. Here's the story of how he decided to quit promoting beer:

Football great Bubba Smith has sworn off booze. Not drinking it, but selling it. Bubba never did drink, but he sold a ton of beer by making cute television ads. Not anymore. Bubba has kicked the habit. As far as I know, Bubba Smith is the first athlete ever, maybe the first person ever, to give up a very lucrative, stupendously easy and really amusing job making beer commercials, just because he decided it was wrong.

Here's how it happened. "I went back to Michigan State for the homecoming parade last year," Bubba said. "I was the grand marshal and I was riding in the back seat of this car. The people were yelling, but they weren't saying, 'Go, State, go!' One side of the street was yelling, 'Tastes great!' and the other side was yelling, 'Less filling.'

Then we go to the stadium. The older folks are yelling, 'Kill, Bubba, kill.' But the students are yelling, 'Tastes great! Less filling!' Everyone in the stands is drunk. It was like I was contributing to alcohol, and I don't drink. It made me realize I was doing something I didn't want to do.

I was with my brother, Tody, who is my agent. I told him, 'Tody, I'll never do another Lite beer commercial.' I loved doing the commercials, but I didn't like the effect it was having on a lot of little people. I'm talking about people in school. Kids would come up to me on the street and recite lines from my commercials, verbatim. They knew the lines better than I did. It was scary. Kids start to listen to things you say; you want to tell 'em something that is the truth.

Doing those commercials, it's like me telling everyone in school, 'Hey, it's cool to have a Lite beer.' I'd go to places like Daytona Beach and Fort Lauderdale on spring breaks (as a spokesman for the brewery), and it was scary to see how drunk those kids were. It was fun talking to the fans, until you see people lying on the beach because they can't make it back to their rooms, or tearing up a city.

As the years wear on, you stop compromising your principles."[2]

### Believers vs. Make Believers

Webster's 1828 Dictionary defines conviction as, "The act of convincing of sin or sinfulness, the state of being convicted by conscience." Also, "The act of compelling one to acknowledge truth." Convictions are deeper than mere preferences. They make you certain of strong beliefs. You won't just acknowledge truth, you will implement it in your life.

Thousands of men felt a fascination and affection for Jesus. But when they heard a call for commitment, most of them split. Jesus was such a Man of conviction that He looked at the last twelve and said (to paraphrase Him), "Go, too, if you want, because these standards aren't going to change." Convictions equal strong beliefs. They won't bend to the winds of peer pressure, shifting social standards, or an "everybody's-doing-it" mentality. They'll get stronger.

Convictions are how you get saved. Believing in Jesus Christ means developing a conviction that He is the only way to heaven. Just believing that this is true, though, doesn't make you saved, no more than standing in a barn makes you a horse. John 1:12 says, "But as many as received Him, to them He gave the right to become children of God, *even to those who believe in His name*" (italics added).

The original Greek text for "believe in" means "believe on." The importance of this phrase expands the point John was trying to make.

- "Believe in" merely agrees with fact. I may "know" the president of the United States, meaning his policies and public appearances. Yet I don't *know* him; we don't have a personal relationship. Acknowledging his presence doesn't make us companions. Likewise, knowing about Jesus doesn't mean you know Him personally. Just believing that He exists won't take you one step closer to heaven.

- "Believe on" implies that, in addition to the facts, you yield your will and affections as you rely on Christ for salvation. In other words, you believe so strongly you feel compelled to humbly obey His Word and follow in His ways.

In talking about total commitment, I like to use the example of a chair. I ask people, "Do you believe the chair at the table will support you?" They respond, "Sure." I follow with, "Why do you *believe* that chair will support you?" They list reasons like it's sturdy, it has four legs, or they have seen someone else sitting in the same type chair. I add, "But why isn't it supporting you right now?" The obvious reply, "Because I'm not sitting in it right now."

So it is with Jesus. You can see Him from a distance, see others seated in Him, and believe all about His plans. But unless you pick yourself up, go over and sit in Him, relying on Him to hold you up, you really won't *know* Him. The reason the church has suffered with inefficiency and been mocked by so much compromise is so many believe in Jesus. But few believe on Him with strong convictions to obey His will.

James 1:6–8 talks about the man who lacks convictions. It refers to him as "double minded" and "unstable in all his ways." The answer for this kind of gutlessness comes from James 4:7–8, "Submit therefore to God. Resist the devil and he will flee from you. Draw near to God and He will draw near to you. Cleanse your hands, you sinners; and purify your hearts, you double minded."

As you humbly come before God, grace comes into your life, giving you strength so you can resist the devil and all of his temptations. Notice, though, in verse 7, that *submit* comes before *resist*. As you submit to God's Word, you begin to develop godly convictions by which you can resist the devil. Hard work. Yet profitable!

### Stand or Fall

There is an old saying that goes, "If you don't stand for something, you will fall for anything." Another calls conviction a belief that you hold on to, or rather it holds you. The difference between a prejudice and a conviction is that you can explain the latter without getting angry. During the rest of this chapter I will discuss men of conviction versus men of preference. Convictions help "long term" people stick it out. The others will drop out of the race.

One of the strongest, toughest men I know is Reggie White of the Green Bay Packers, the "Minister of Defense." Though an all-pro ever since he entered the NFL, even stronger than his physical depth are Reggie's personal values. They come from being a disciple of Jesus Christ. His convictions are so rooted in God's Word that, as he puts it, "Talking about my relationship with Jesus Christ is as natural for me as breathing."

Such strong convictions cause you to "put up or shut up." Like Reggie. Here's his story:

I was playing in a controlled scrimmage against the Detroit Lions one hot, muggy summer day in Detroit. I had outmaneuvered a frustrated Detroit rookie for most of the day from my left defensive end position. Then our helmets accidentally locked together on a play.

This guy used foul language that I would not let my dogs hear. I can take losing a game, but I cannot tolerate being cussed out to my face.

I looked him right in the eye and announced, "Jesus is coming back soon, and I hope you're ready." But he just tossed more choice words into my face and returned to his huddle. I was angry. Again I shouted to him across the field, "Jesus is coming back soon, and I hope you're ready."

My teammates were urging me back to our defensive huddle. But instead I eyeballed this rookie and shouted to my teammates, "Jesus is coming back soon, and I hope he's ready."

The next play, I lined up in front of the same rookie and said, "Jesus is coming back soon, and *I don't think you're ready.*"

The ball snapped and I announced, "Here comes Jesus!"

I thrust my entire 285-pound body right into his chest and drove him back about five yards. He plopped to the turf just in time to see me sack his quarterback. My teammates and coach often asked after that if Jesus was coming back on the next play!

I'm still not sure why I said what I did that steamy day in Detroit. Maybe it was the heat. Maybe it was his language. Maybe it was just my desire to live my life glorifying Jesus Christ.[3]

It took more than size to make that kind of stand. It took strength and courage . . . the same type displayed by power forward A.C. Green at an "Athletes for Abstinence" rally at a Southern California high school. He told the students: "There was a lot of pressure from my teammates . . . to have sex 'cause to them it was a natural thing . . . it was important for me to be part of the home boys, but what was even more important was the respect I had for myself."[4]

Christian convictions are the trademark of true believers. They act like barbed wire placed around a pure heart. When believers mix that protection with faith in Jesus, they can obtain the victory. Of course, when I speak of convictions, I mean those that are biblically-based. Jesus was a man of principles, which came from the convictions He received from His Father. All our convictions must follow His ideals and model His standards.

Ed Cole points out in his book, *Real Man,* the danger of not holding to standards: "Today, moral principles inherent in God's Word still form the only true value system that sustains life and makes societies worthwhile. Rejection of absolutes makes all rules and regulations relative and slated to the self-interests of the powerful."[5]

The modern-day, value-less system makes it that much more important for believers to stand on convictions based on God's Word. The support structures of our character comes from the pillars of our convictions. They build our character and decide our fate. Following Jesus is a walk of faith based on the convictions we hold. Hebrews 11:1 says, "Now faith is the assurance of things hoped for, the *conviction* of things not seen" (italics added). Faith and convictions go hand in hand.

## Convictions vs. Preferences

Some people have the faith of a sand castle. When the first wave of problems, adversity, and pressure hits, they wash away. You can't find a trace of faith in them. But convictions add bedrock to the building of your faith (read Matt. 7:24–27). Convictions are absolute, unchangeable beliefs, regardless of circumstances. They don't allow for compromise.

Pastor A.R. Bernard, of Brooklyn, New York, taught me the difference between convictions and preference.

1. People who live by preference can be negotiated out of their preferences. Convictions are non-negotiable.

2. People who live by preferences weaken under pressure. Those with conviction grow stronger.

3. People who live by preference always dislike those who hold convictions.[6]

## Deadly Preference

Men of preference are the worst hypocrites and can do the most damage. When you live a life of preference, you are not only damaging your character, you may be preventing others from entering into God's kingdom as well. Take the following example.

Years ago in Germany, a young Jewish boy had a profound sense of admiration for his father. The family's life centered on acts of piety and devotion prescribed by their religion. Zealous in attending worship services and instruction, the father demanded the same of his children. However, when the boy became a teenager, the family was forced to move to another town where there was no synagogue. All the pillars of society belonged to the Lutheran church. Suddenly the father announced they were abandoning their Jewish traditions to become Lutherans. When the stunned family asked why, the father explained it was necessary to help his business.

Bewildered and confused, the youngster's deep disappointment soon gave way to anger and intense bitterness that plagued him throughout his life. He left Germany to study in England. Each day at the British museum, he formulated his ideas and composed a book. In it, he introduced a new life and world view and conceived a movement designed to change the world. Not surprisingly, he described religion as an "opiate for the masses" and insisted everything turned on economics. Over the years, billions of people suffered under the system invented by this embittered man, the infamous Karl Marx. The influence of his father's lack of conviction is still keenly felt around the world.[7]

But Marx is not simply an isolated figure of history. There are millions of Christian men today who live by preference, not conviction. They negotiate and compromise with the world's system. Unable to stand by tough decisions, they sway with their emotions and give in to circumstances.

The true test of the strength of your convictions is measured by the strength of your opposition. Quit grumbling about spiritual trials and temptations. View the devil's schemes as God's barbells, giving you a spiritual workout to build massive faith muscles. Convictions will govern your actions and subdue your fleshly opposition to truth and righteousness.

Many people call the conscience the voice of God. No, your conscience is a gift from God. With those who lack conviction, a clear conscience is only a poor memory. When a man won't listen to his conscience, it's usually because he doesn't want advice from a stranger! Convictions are our greatest allies in securing peace and lasting happiness.

### Men of Conviction

Can you be a man of conviction? It's possible through God's power. Consider some men who were.

- First and foremost, the Lord Jesus. Out of His sense of mission from the heavenly Father, He spoke words of conviction in the Sermon on the Mount. The multitudes were amazed at His authority and followed Him (Matt. 7:29).

- Moses. His convictions were a sign of spiritual maturity. Hebrews 11:24–26 recalls how Moses, when he had grown to manhood, refused to be called a son of Pharaoh's daughter.

Instead, he sided with the abused and mistreated slaves of Israel; it was better to be on God's side than enjoy passing pleasures.

- Joseph. He never gave up hope or excused his actions because he was an innocent victim. He stood morally pure, fleeing the seduction of Potiphar's wife (Gen. 37–45.) In prison Joseph stood on God's promises. He became Pharaoh's right-hand man and the avenue of salvation to God's chosen people.

- Daniel. He proved you can live a noncompromising devotion to God in the midst of a compromising world. Daniel 1:8 describes how he made up his mind to not defile himself with unclean food that was unlawful for Israelites to eat. Daniel and his friends faced more than one life-threatening situation because they refused to bend to Babylon's ways. The convictions he held established the purpose of his life.

## Application

While all convictions must be based on the Word of God, the convictions you live by must be yours. Romans 14:22a says, "The faith which you have, have as your own conviction before God." In other words, you can't hold to my convictions, your pastor's, or your parents. You can't follow them just because someone else said you must do so. You have to adopt them as yours. Otherwise, your faith will suffer a shipwreck (1 Tim. 1:19).

When it comes to issues like holiness, daily Bible reading, dating, and your walk with God, you will follow only His ways if you develop strong convictions about them. Just having understanding doesn't guarantee success. A great example is the knowledge contained on cigarette packs. I would like to see the Surgeon General's warning reworded to say: "Warning! You dummy! These things will kill you!" Yet millions smoke them anyway. (And remember, the cigarette smokes. You're just the sucker.) Your motivation must be rooted in something deeper than mere knowledge.

Peter saw the supernatural feeding of thousands, the dead raised to life, blind eyes opened, healings of major disease, devils cast out, and the transfiguration of Christ. He also was the first disciple to receive the supernatural revelation that Jesus was the Christ, the Son of God. Yet none of this knowledge sustained his faith the night he denied Jesus three times. Knowledge must be cultivated by faith, and faith must be cultivated by convictions. Then convictions will be developed and undergird your destiny. The devil can't whip a man who stands on God-given convictions.

Read about Abraham in Romans 4:20–22. This is a perfect picture of a man of conviction:

- "He did not waver in unbelief." He was not double-minded.

- "But grew strong." His faith matured.

- "Giving glory to God." His priorities were in the right place.

- "Being fully assured." He trusted God's promises.

- "It was reckoned to him as righteousness." He received the promise.

Developing convictions means entering a new way of life, a disciplined, God-honoring lifestyle. Convictions open the locker room door and admit you to the playing field as a Christian contender, making you ready to fight the good fight of faith. It is your induction into Jesus' training routine. Convictions call for living consistently and unselfishly, developing habits until they become reflex actions in times of temptation, oppression, fear, and confrontation.

Dare to step out and develop convictions to help you defeat shortcomings and difficulties in your life. It's not a crime to goof up now and then. It's only a crime if you never start. Defeat should never be a source of discouragement, but a push to succeed the next time. Are you ready to go for it? Good, because now you have to learn to develop the backbone to fight the biggest battle of your life: having pure relationships with women. Read on.

### Gut Check

1. Make a list of your "Top Ten Convictions" (unchangeable beliefs.) For example, "Jesus Christ is the Lord of my life," or, "I will not sexually defile myself before marriage." Convictions will be-

come the bedrock of your faith and a "safety net" for your righteousness.

2. What are the "secret" sins that keep tripping you up? List them.

3. Has there been a time when you had to stand for your convictions, your faith? What happened?

4. Does absolute truth exist? What is truth based on? (See Ps. 119:160 and John 14:6.)

5. We are all going to make mistakes from time to time. Even King David, "the apple of God's eye," made serious errors.

a. What was David's response when he was confronted with his sin? (See 2 Sam. 11–12 and Ps. 51:1–17.)

b. What should our response be when we are confronted with our sin or compromise? (See 2 Cor. 7:9–11, 1 John 1:9 and Philippians 3:12–14.) List the biblical answers.

# 7

## BEAUTY AND THE BEAST

*He who finds a wife finds a good thing, and obtains favor from the Lord.*

*—Proverbs 18:22*

EVER HEAR THE FUNNY STORY ABOUT ADAM and his perfect match? Adam was standing in the Garden of Eden with his Heavenly Father one day. He asked: "God, why did you make Eve so beautiful? I mean, she's got the softest skin, voluptuous figure, long silky hair, and radiant eyes. It's so incredible!"

"Well, son," God said as He looked knowingly at Adam, "that's so you would be attracted to her."

"Oh, I get it," Adam smiled. Then he rubbed his head, looked inquisitively at the Lord and asked, "But why did you make her so stupid?"

"Oh, that's easy," God said. "That was so she would be attracted to you."

Laugh a minute. Then think about romance. Ah, sweet love. What could be wrong with that? Plenty. Romance has been *the* idol of the younger generation for more than a decade. I know. Before I turned away from parties, lust, and premarital sex, I *craved* it. And, millions of young men think that finding the "woman of their dreams" will fill the emotional void in their lives. *Not!*

As a young teenager, I became obsessed with the imagined need for a girlfriend. That set a pattern that continued into my early twenties. It may be the same one trapping you. Back in eighth grade, I had my heart set on meeting a certain cheerleader, so desperately it tainted my zeal for playing football. Lacking self-confidence and (so I thought) peer acceptance, I thought a wonderful relationship with that "special" girl would make my life complete. What a fantasy! I needed to fall in love with Jesus. He's the one who gave me acceptance, security, and masculine identity, and perfectly pieced my life together as if He were solving a puzzle.

I have talked about lordship. Well, you haven't given God anything until you give Him your affections and emotions. Under the Lordship of Jesus, you want to please Him. That means you can't throw away your love and affection on any girl with a pretty face, hot body, or nice legs. Ask the Lord if He wants you to invest your time with this woman. This differs from the Christian dating game played in most church youth groups. Too many follow the worldly pattern of test-driving the latest model. It reminds me of "mall cruisers" who want to shop around.

Without the Lord's blessing, the outcome of such relationships is pretty grim. Let's face it, 99 percent of casual dating fails, leading to heartbreak and the scars of rejection. There has to be a better way! The Lord didn't intend for you to fumble through one relationship to the next so that you ultimately wind up carrying a load of emotional baggage to the altar. God doesn't want previous intimate relationships or one-night affairs haunting your marriage.

## Courtship, Not Dating

Young men, do you think you're impressing the ladies with your intelligence, abilities, power, and imitations of the latest movie star or rock musician? I doubt it. It's probably more like the girl who told me: "Dating is just like 'tug of war.' One big jerk after another."

Dating is more of a wash-out than most people believe, but only because they seldom hear how the opposite sex feels. That is why I believe in the principles of courtship, not random dating. Courtship is when two mature people of the opposite sex feel attracted to each other. They feel that, potentially, their relationship could lead to matrimony. It requires asking, "God, is this Your will?" Unlike the casual, social dating scene, this calls for a high degree of sensitivity and seriousness.

The key word here is *time.* Don't rush it! Relationships best mature through group fellowships and social events. Then, after prayer and wise counsel (from your parents, pastor, or other responsible adult), you and your prospective spouse choose to enter courtship. Never start without guidelines: Should we allow kissing? Can we kiss without it leading to other behavior? What other situations should we avoid? Do we need a curfew?

Right now you may be shaking your head and saying: "Give me a break. That's not real." Wrong again. When my wife and I were engaged, we knew ten other Christian couples who wound up hitting the sack before they made it to the altar. They didn't take any precautions and their bodies overcame their good intentions. That is why I advise young couples never to go behind closed doors alone. For two reasons:

- Even the strongest believer can fall to lust. Joseph ran away from Potiphar's wife when she wanted him to come to bed (see Gen. 39). Not because he was super spiritual. He knew that if he didn't run, the pressure would get to him. After all, the rulers in Egypt had their pick of beautiful women when it came to selecting a wife.

- First Thessalonians 5:21–22 says to avoid even the appearance of evil. I know dozens of young couples who, because they aren't having sex, think it's "cool" to spend the night in each other's beds. Then they wonder why others accuse them of immorality. Or, take the lady who was shocked when players from the Los Angeles Raiders called her a whore. She protested that all she was doing was witnessing to some of them. *Where* was the problem—in their hotel rooms. Naturally, people assumed the worst.

Courtship is the prelude to engagement. Its goals are to honor God, maintain a high degree of holiness and—this is especially crucial—minimize emotional trauma if the relationship turns sour. There is no shame in being wrong. Yet, it's always better to walk away with integrity intact. And if you're wrong, that woman will become another man's wife. Don't you dare take something that is not yours! Namely, her physical and emotional love.

## Miss Right

In this chapter, I will give you some guidelines for successful courtship and interaction with our sisters in the Lord. I also will share how I found my gift from God, my wife, Dana. I hope it will stir you, by example, to join the men who have displayed the willingness to trust the Lord in this matter.

It's often easier to trust Jesus for our salvation than to help us find the perfect mate. Suddenly we think He surely needs our help. (After all, no guy wants a girl with that "faraway" look: the farther away she is, the better she looks.) Wrong! Read about Isaac and Rebekkah in Genesis 24. God directed the selection of Isaac's wife, and his first reaction was, "He loved her" (verse 67).

God wishes to repeat the story of Isaac and Rebekkah in the lives of young men and women around the world. But you must submit to His will. To have this kind of marriage, you must totally trust and believe in God's perfect understanding. Hard? Of course. But in return, you will get His best. Don't settle for less.

God knows what He's doing! He knows the desires of your heart and what makes you tick. There is someone God created to walk by your side. She will be the perfect match for you. Adam and Eve didn't have to date to see if they were compatible. God brought them together. If you follow His plan, He will do the same for you. There is a girl out there who is just right for you.

After all, God's judgment is perfect. He knows who He has called you to join in nuptial ties before you were even born. So He has already selected your wife, unless you have received the gift of celibacy (doubtful for most of you). So quit worrying. When the time is right, He will do it.

## My Story

In days gone by, when I was a lukewarm Christian, I constantly found myself discredited in dating relationships because of lust. Like a mouse wandering into a trap baited with Swiss cheese, I fell for it every time. Thankfully, when I genuinely gave my heart to Christ, a pastor prayed that I would be free of it. I'll never forget his words of encouragement: "Tom, God has a girl picked out for you. She's perfect and holy. But if you want that type of girl, you'll have to be that type of man."

I thank God for the pastors and other men who have given me such godly counsel in my life. That day I made a commitment to treat women like fine china: No fingerprints! I vowed that the next time I said, "I love you," I would follow up with the question, "Will you marry me?" That hung a high price tag on those three little words. I used to toss them around like a frisbee. No more.

For the next three years I didn't date, touch, or kiss a woman. Tough? Sure. But I was holding out for God's best. Once I thought I would marry a certain girl, but didn't. At least neither of us walked away with a broken heart. No contact, no fouls!

One day I shared my testimony at a Christian men's meeting that aired on a local radio station. A young woman, Dana Cody, was listening. She got so excited about college students who were serious about serving the Lord that she came down to meet us. When I saw her, one word came to mind: gorgeous!!! No wonder she was Miss California. (Since we're now married, I guess that makes me Mr. California.)

A new Christian, Dana wanted to attend college in Southern California. Naturally, I suggested USC. I told her to call if she wanted me to show her around the campus, where I had begun working in ministry full time after graduation. Three months passed. Zippo. I pretty much forgot her. Little did I know that one day she would see the man who led me to the Lord on Christian TV. Rice Broocks was talking about a reformed "wild man" who was shaking up USC's campus. When he mentioned my name, Dana grabbed my business card, thinking: "That guy wasn't just trying to pick me up. He was legit."

She called and I got her tickets to the big football game with our arch rival, UCLA. Afterward, we attended the Saturday night fellowship at my church. Since my alma mater lost, I felt a little low. Yet I had a strange feeling that I would win something bigger than a football game, namely, Dana's heart.

Hungering for God, she fell in love with our church's vision (training Christian leaders to impact the world with the gospel) long before she loved me. We became close friends over the next three years. We worked together on campus outreaches and talked at fellowships and church meetings, yet never dated. All that time I wrestled with this thought: *Is she the one?* At one point, I scoffed, *Nah. It'll never happen.*

Finally, after I felt the Lord urging me to "pop the question," I consulted my pastor. When I told him I thought the Lord had said that Dana would be my wife, he joked, "Big Tommy, I think you were just hearing that bad burrito you ate last night." After I punched him on the arm, he said: "You may be on to something. Let's wait and see what happens."

Less than a week later, Dana went to my pastor's wife and said, "I think the Lord spoke to me to marry Tom." Without telling me that, my pastor called to say, "Why don't you go and ask Dana to marry you?" So I set up our first official date at Parker's Lighthouse in Long Beach, a fancy restaurant overlooking the Pacific Ocean. (When I do something, I do it right.)

I have never been so nervous in my life. Combat in the trenches of USC football looked like child's play compared to facing this petite beauty queen over dinner. All day the devil kept whispering, "She's going to laugh in your face, 'Tom, you're as ugly as a mud fence.'" Praise God that love is blind. I hope you're not laughing too hard right now, lest you look in the mirror! (Just kidding, guys.)

Well, as you already know, Dana accepted my proposal, and we were engaged. Are you wondering what happened to courtship? I think it took place between the hors d'oeuvres and the main course. Seriously, over the next ten months we built a close friendship and set the foundation for our ministry together. Until our "I do's" at the altar, we never kissed. Not once. Not that it would have been a terrible sin. Neither great moral strength nor virtue restrained me. Out of fear and reverence for God, though, I drew a line way back from compromise. Even if we stumbled, we would still be in God's good graces.

As I mentioned earlier, I've seen too many Christians fall into vice because they refused to set guidelines or hold to convictions about holiness in premarital relationships. Take the guy who asked me how far he could go with his girlfriend and still be all right in God's sight. I replied: "You big lust dog. What do you mean, 'How far can you go?' I wouldn't trust you to go up the block to McDonald's with her."

Instead of setting a standard on the edge of compromise, why not set it as far away from that line as possible? If you walk close to the edge, it's too easy to fall prey to the devil. When I drew a line, I didn't stop there. We asked some close friends and pastors to check up on us. We wanted to be accountable for our actions. That proved a great encouragement and strength.

Well, we made it! And at the altar, when we enjoyed our first kiss, it was all worth it. What an explosion! I have never regretted abstaining from premarital relations. We both take great delight in having a clean conscience from our courtship, and our marital vows have taken on a much deeper significance than if we had decided a little "fooling around" ahead of time wouldn't hurt.

Years later, at the wedding of some close friends, they used all Disney love songs in their ceremony. Dana looked at me and said: "Tom, we should have thought about Disney love songs. Then we could have used 'Beauty and the Beast.'" What a sense of humor!

## Dating Principles

Date. It rhymes with mate, which means, "one joined with another." Dating naturally leads to mating. That is why the subject deserves to be treated much more seriously than it is in the casual social scene of the nineties. You also need some guideposts in order to glorify the Lord in your relationships with the opposite sex.

Nowhere in the Bible can you find the word *dating*. Some call it a grey area, since the Bible doesn't directly address the issue. Still, there are verses that apply to interaction with women. They will guide your conduct and rule your behavior. If you allow the Lord to govern your relationships, you will be blessed and will prosper socially. Ignore Him, and your chances of misery will be like a rigged poker game: a sure bet!

*1. Hebrews 13:4: "Let marriage be held in honor among all, and let the marriage bed be undefiled; for fornicators and adulterers God will judge."*

This Scripture is a reference for before and after marriage. Sex, an act reserved for marriage, is a sign from God between a man and woman. Romantic love is the highest expression of intimacy and seals the marital covenant. This special union is to be shared only by husband and wife. Therefore, sex outside marriage is dishonorable, forbidden, and immoral.

Since sex consummates the marriage agreement, God looks on premarital sex and extra-marital sex as vile and immoral. For a young man to engage in premarital sex with a partner who is not, and never will be, his partner means he has violated another man's wife. He has disgraced the institution of marriage. Even engaged couples must wait. You should not begin a lifelong commitment having dishonored the sacredness of your marriage bed. When the time arrives for physical love, it will be of much greater value. That will make it even more special.

*2. First Thessalonians 5:21–22: "But examine everything carefully; hold fast to that which is good; abstain from every form [appearance] of evil."*

To help you remain honest, find someone else to hold you accountable for the standards of your relationship. It can be your pastor, youth leader, or parents. Whoever you choose, it should be someone who can hold you accountable. This means you open yourself up for tough questions. Yet, this may save you from hurt, embarrassment, and potential disaster.

*3. First John 2:16: "For all that is in the world, the lust of the flesh and the lust of the eyes and the boastful pride of life, is not from the Father, but is from the world."*

Is your relationship God-ordained or self-started? God's idea or your idea? Judge the fruits, or byproducts, of your relationship carefully (especially if you're already dating someone). The world's dating game relies on appearance and self-satisfaction. These roots grow the rotten kind of fruit seen in our troubled social scene. Heartache, emotional turmoil, sexually-transmitted diseases, and sky-rocketing divorce rates grow from a source of careless, unbiblical dating.

The only thing you take into marriage is your character. If you aren't faithful before, you aren't likely to be faithful afterward. And if your relationship stems from lust, marriage won't cure your problem. If you're a lust hound before marriage, you will continue to be unable to find satisfaction in one, committed relationship. Lust is *never* satisfied.

The time to deal with lust is before you make it to the altar. Left alone, it becomes like a poisonous snake, waiting to destroy you. If your attraction to your wife is primarily physical—good looking legs, nice breasts—you are headed for disaster. As Galatians 6:8a says, "For the one who sows to his own flesh shall from the flesh reap corruption."

Look honestly at your relationship. Is it drawing you closer to Jesus or pushing you away? If you inspect your fruit and see that it's rotten, have the courage to follow Matthew 5:30a, where Jesus says, "If your right hand makes you stumble, cut it off, and throw it from you." Not literally. What He meant was to get away from whatever causes you to sin. Pronto!

*4. First Corinthians 7:1: "Now concerning the things about which you wrote, it is good for a man not to touch a woman."*

In Greek, the word *touch* as it's used here means "to stir to sensuality." In other words, fanning lustful desires you cannot fulfill righteously. Sight primarily stimulates men, but touch arouses women. Too many so-called Christian men are wolves in sheep's clothing, rubbing up to sisters with not-so-holy hugs. If you find yourself in a position where hugging is appropriate, avoid chest-to-chest contact. Hug from the side. As for heated petting—abstain! It stirs up lust and easily goes too far. Consider, too, whether your dress glorifies God or arouses spirits of sensuality and flirting. While you may think of this as a woman's concern, it also applies to guys.

*5. First Corinthians 7:27b: "Are you released from a wife? Do not seek a wife."*

No, this doesn't mean you can never marry. What it says is that finding a mate should not be your life's all-consuming passion. Matthew 6:33 says, "But seek first His kingdom and His righteousness; and all these things shall be added to you." Namely, keep your eyes on God's business and He will take care of your needs. Including marriage. As a disciple of Christ, devote your efforts to personal spiritual growth, maturity, and character. When the time is right, God will bring you the right relationship.

6. *First Corinthians 7:32–35: "But I want you to be free from concern. One who is unmarried is concerned about the things of the Lord, how he may please the Lord; but one who is married is concerned about the things of the world, how he may please his wife, and his interests are divided. And the woman who is unmarried, and the virgin, is concerned about the things of the Lord, that she may be holy both in body and in spirit; but one who is married is concerned about the things of the world, how she may please her husband. And this I say for your own benefit; not to put restraint upon you, but to promote what is seemly, and to secure undistracted devotion to the Lord."*

The object of this passage is to instruct Christians in acting properly and "secure undistracted devotion to the Lord." Judging by my evangelistic experience, one of the devil's top tricks is to trip up new converts with a woman. I can't count the number of young men I've watched fall away from God because their dream girl "miraculously" appeared on the scene, only to bring them to complete ruin.

One young man I knew offers a vivid example. Our ministry had begun working on a campus in southern California. The star quarterback was one of our first converts. This promising athlete had incredible stature and a strong call from God on his life. Shortly after he accepted Jesus into his heart, a woman (I believe one sent from the pit of hell) claiming to be a Christian seduced him. He got her pregnant; she had an abortion. In turn, he quit the football team, and started running from God as fast as he could. Where is he today? In a coffin with half his head blown away. On the Wednesday night he should have been in our Bible study, he was in the wrong place at the wrong time and fell victim to senseless violence. Distracted devotion cost this young man his life. I'm not trying to scare you into commitment. Yet you need to be aware of Satan's schemes. Don't get trapped.

7. *First Timothy 5:2 which says to treat "the younger women as sisters, in all purity."*

The cute Christian girl you've got your eye on? She is one of God's daughters, a member of the Christian family, your sister in Christ. Though you may go as far as engagement in your commitment, you do not "own title" to her. She is your sister and must remain that way until you marry. How would you treat your earthly sister? Would you French kiss her? (Ugh! I hope not.) Maybe that sounds too graphic, but I'm serious. You have no right to any woman's body or her unreserved affections until you tie the marriage knot. Your actions must be acceptable in the spirit of your mutual Father, who is God.

"Okay," you say, "but I'm just an ordinary guy, man, with natural urges." Right. We all are. And the battle doesn't end just because you get married. If you're thinking of taking that step—or already have—you'll want to continue on to chapter 8.

## Gut Check

1. Are you dating a "special" woman right now? If you answered yes, evaluate that relationship.

a. Have you offered your relationship to God in prayer to see if it is His will for your life? Remember, if Jesus is the Lord of your life, He calls the shots over your emotions and romance.

b. How has your relationship drawn you closer to Jesus or pushed you farther away?

c. What does the Bible say about relationships that are born of the flesh (physical desires)? See Romans 8:5–8 and Galatians 6:7–9.

d. What are your personal guidelines or standards you have set to preserve a relationship that will be pleasing to Jesus?

e. Do you have someone you can go to who will keep you accountable for purity in this relationship? If not, find someone. When Dana and I were dating, in the back of mind I knew my pastor would ask me the next week whether I compromised my standards. Knowing he would hold me accountable served as a godly restraint.

2. Generally speaking, should a Christian ever date or be engaged to a non-believer? (See 2 Cor. 6:14–18).

3. What does sex symbolize to you? Why do you think God put guidelines on the use of sex? (Read all of Prov. 5 and 7.)

4. Do you struggle with looking at women more as sex symbols than as sisters created by God? If you answered yes, how can you change your thinking? (See Ps. 119:9, Rom. 12:1–2). Write down some solutions.

*8*

# NOW THAT I GOT HER, WHAT DO I DO WITH HER?

*Marriage used to be a contract. Now many regard it as a 90-day option.*

—*Anonymous*[1]

A COLLEGE MAN WALKED INTO A photography studio with a framed picture of his girlfriend. He wanted the picture duplicated. This involved removing it from the frame. In doing this, the studio owner noticed the inscription on the back of the photograph: 'My dearest Tom, I love you with all my heart. I love you more and more each day. I will love you forever and ever. I am yours for all eternity.' It was signed, 'Diane,' and it contained a P.S.: 'If we ever break up, I want this picture back.'

"We who have been baptized have professed our love for God and for others. We belong to Christ. There can be no P.S. in our life given to God. We can never break up with Him. We are His. We belong to Him—forever."[2]

Marriage is the mirror of our relationship to God. In Genesis 2:24, God said a man and woman come together and become one flesh. In God's eyes, that leaves no room for, "In case this doesn't work out, let's sign a prenuptial agreement." God intends for us to spend the rest of our lives with the partner He favors us with; not only does that mean a lifelong partnership, but also it means you don't "own" your wife. You are, however, to carefully guard her affections.

When Dana and I married, I never dreamed God would use her to smoke out my selfishness, bad habits, and ungodly attitudes. Marriage proved to be the very thing I needed to step into new stature as a man and a more mature commitment to Christ.

Looking back on single life, being a good Christian was easy. I never had to worry about checking my desires to serve someone else. Single and independent, I ate when I wanted, went wherever and whenever I wanted, and stayed as long as I felt like it. A weekly group discipleship meeting was the only time I submitted to someone else's schedule. Don't misunderstand. I was under the lordship of Jesus. Yet, much of the time the main person I worried about was me.

Marriage is like being born again. It calls for dying to self and coming to life in a new relationship. You must be willing to give up single life for married life. It is worth it. But marriage carries a price tag. I thought I was ready, but, truthfully, I wasn't. I thought I could "beat the system" and enjoy the best of both worlds. Wrong!

When Genesis 2:24 says a man shall "cleave" to his wife, that means to pursue her actively and choose her above all others. Don't be like the man who chases his bride to the wedding altar, then sets her on the trophy shelf of his ego. He pays attention to her occasionally to meet his selfish need for pleasure. But he ignores her emotional needs, and neglects their relationship until a once-hot romance turns ice cold. Or as mystery novelist Agatha Christie once said, "An archeologist is the best husband a wife can have. The older she gets, the more interested he is in her."[3]

## See Ya Later, Babe

Two weeks after my honeymoon, this he-man had had enough feminine floweriness and romance to last a long time. Thanks to my ignorance and insensitivity, one day I sharply announced, "Honey, I hope you can understand this . . . I gotta get out with the men."

Big mistake! True, I needed some masculine fellowship. We all do, just as wives need the company of other women. But my heavy-handed approach left a lot to be desired. I could see the hurt etched deeply in her eyes. She needed to know whether I cared about her more than my male friends.

I'm not particularly proud of that moment. Yet I know I am not alone. Many men make similar blunders. They neglect their wife and children, selfishly putting their interests ahead of her and family. You know the excuses:

- "Don't bother me right now, honey, the game's on."

- "I've been under a lot of pressure lately. Quit bugging me."

- "I'm going hunting (or fishing) this weekend with the guys. You don't expect me to paint the bathroom, too, do you?"

- "We're going out to bowl a few games and grab a bite to eat. We won't be gone long."

You may have a legitimate need to watch a game, relax, blow off a little steam, and build friendships. But not at your wife's expense. Are you one of those men who scratches your head, wondering why your wife won't respond to your romantic advances, or why she constantly nags you? Maybe it's because you don't put her intimate needs and desires above yours. If she knows the affirmation of your love, and that she ranks first on your list (after God), she won't resent you spending time with friends.

Women have a much greater need for communication than men. Not a few minutes of gab about what happened at the office, but time to express deep-felt needs and exchange feelings, hopes, and dreams. Years later, I am still growing and learning in this area. After all, marriage is the art of two incompatible people learning to live with each other.

It may not be popular to say this, but the overwhelming responsibility for marriage leadership falls with the man. The call to marriage will challenge you to change. Embrace it instead of fighting it like I did. Either you will change or your marriage will dissolve. The first may seem unpleasant. The second will prove dreadful.

Single life was so easy. After an exhilarating night on the town, I dropped Dana off on her front porch, said good night and went my merry way. After marriage, it was through the door together. Suddenly she was around twenty-four hours a day, seven days a week. What a change! Not only did we get to see each other at our best, we had to stand each other at our worst. She looked different without makeup. She didn't always smell "pepperminty" fresh, especially in the morning. Neither did I.

Don't laugh, men, you aren't always in perfect form. You may brag that you are "cock-a-doodle-do" fresh in the morning. More likely you look like a groggy-eyed robin pulling up worms. You may have impressed your fiance with your masculine, well-groomed appearance on dates, when you were always on your best behavior. You were the prince of attentiveness, courtesy, and gentlemanly behavior. You treated her like a queen. But after the honeymoon she got stuck with the *real you*. If your mate is unhappy, you need to take a hard look in the mirror.

### Life with the Bear

Hollywood fantasies fuel unrealistic expectations and images of marital bliss. They did ours. It reminds me of the saying, "The difference between courtship and marriage is the difference between the pictures in the seed catalog and what comes up."[4]

Dana couldn't wait to sleep all night long in the tender, romantic embrace of her hunk as we cuddled the night away. That lasted until the first night of our honeymoon when I snored like a bear in hibernation, and she woke up with a crick in her neck from lying on my chest, which was much higher off the bed than she expected. I fantasized about a never-ending love affair filled with romance and intimacy. What I got was a nerve-wracking bout filled with more bills, dirty diapers, and failure to communicate than one man could bear.

We can laugh about these problems now since the worst is behind us. But the root of my problem was in lack of responsibility. I wasn't ready to assume my position as the head of a household. During our first year together I remember muttering: "God, You tricked me into this. You made me love sick. No one ever told me marriage was so tough. I didn't sign up for this."

As I discovered, marriage was like twirling a baton, flipping cartwheels, or eating with chopsticks. It looks easy until you try it! But God wanted me to grow up, embrace change, and step into a higher level of Christian service, one I didn't reach as a single man.

There is a big difference between fantasy and reality. Fantasy is the four-color poster on the wall of the fast-food restaurant. Reality sits on your plate. And the moment I said, "I do," to my beautiful bride, I bit into reality. That meant accepting a great responsibility, to her and as the father of our children.

The humorous side of the picture came when I asked Dana's father for her hand in marriage. After he nodded his approval, he added, "I just hope you make enough money to support her hair and cosmetics." (Which is still difficult.) Funny, maybe, but serious, too. For those of you who are still single, remember that your love's habits, desires, needs, and wants will become yours, too.

Too many young men don't have the first clue about the enormous responsibility they accept by asking for a woman's hand in marriage. It is so serious that God's Word addresses it. First Timothy 5:8 puts it this way: "But if any one does not provide for his own, and especially for those of his household, he has denied the faith, and is worse than an unbeliever."

For men who want to be leaders, Paul lays out these qualifications in 1 Timothy 3:4–5: "He must be one who manages his own household well, keeping his children under control with all dignity (but if a man does not know how to manage his own household, how will he take care of the church of God?)"

Whether you are a church leader or member, these are wise guidelines for those who want to set a godly example for our society. But, providing for your family and managing your household consist of more than giving them food, clothing, and shelter. You must serve as the head of the house to provide spiritual covering (prayer), Bible and devotional studies, and upholding standards of good conduct. You are the priest of your home. As husband and father, you are the "point man" leading your family into the future.

Ignoring your duties leaves your wife in an insecure environment. Without a sense of security she will usurp your authority and start to "wear the pants." That will be unhealthy for everyone, particularly for you, the husband. You lose much-needed respect to properly guide, guard, and govern your family. The roots of the word *husband* come from "house" and "bond." The husband is to be the authoritative voice bonding the house together.

## Missing Men

Last year, I saw Tulsa pastor Carlton Pearson on a TV program, preaching from Ezekiel 22:30: "And I searched for a man among them who should build up the wall and stand in the gap before Me for the land, that I should not destroy it; but I found no one." He went on to stress the need for more men to stand in the gap for America, which requires men to *lead* their families, not just be passive figures in the home. "When a man is not in his proper place," Pearson said, "the woman becomes displaced, the children become misplaced and God becomes replaced."

This is too often the disastrous pattern. I know that men are failing to discipline as I watch their children at church act up, run around, yell, and throw ferocious tantrums if they don't get their own way. Meanwhile, their fathers stand by passively, acting as if nothing is wrong.

Whether you are a prospective marriage partner, young husband, or new father, the key word for your future is *responsibility*, defined as obliged to account (for), answerable (to), involving obligations or duties, dependable. But my favorite goes like this: "Respond-ability." I define that as the ability to act or take charge of a specific need, or react to a specific challenge or situation.

Modern divorce statistics show that too many men cave in to the pressures of family life and other difficulties, bailing out at the first sign of trouble. They are men without any backbone, men who have developed sunken chests. It takes respond-ability to mature through the continuing challenges of married life.

## The Big Five

There are five areas in which married men need the ability to respond and show themselves as "house-bond" husbands. Your list may be a little different or a little longer. But I rate these as the most important:

*Responsibility #1: You are to be the steward (caretaker) of your wife's affections.*

Your wife is your help mate. Ephesians 5:22 says she is to submit to her husband, not be dominated by him. You are not to "lord over" your authority on her. You must honor her as a co-heir with Jesus. Submissiveness means she stands by your side, not under your feet. The wedding ring is symbolic of your never-ending love for each other, not a shackle that binds her to you.

People describe marriage as a 50-50 partnership. More properly, it is 100-100, where you willingly lay down your life for each other, giving preference to the other person's needs. As a man you never—I repeat, never—have the right to abuse your wife, verbally or physically, for any reason. Only insecure men who doubt their masculinity resort to this kind of treatment. A real man is someone who lovingly cherishes his wife and builds her self-esteem.

Ephesians 5:25 commands men, "Husbands, love your wives, just as Christ also loved the church and gave Himself up for her." This verse is not merely a good idea. It is a divine order. I first heard this statement at Ed Cole's meetings and it sank deep into my spirit: Love centers in a man's will. It is not merely an emotion. You can will to love your wife.

As a young, married man, this was one of the toughest lessons I ever learned. Given a pair of stubborn, often volatile personalities, we were headed for serious clashes. After I hurt Dana with my words, she would reject or disrespect me. Then I allowed bitterness, anger, and grudges to swell up in my heart. While my ministry was thriving, my home life was in shambles. I knew I could lose my wife, our son, and my credibility as an evangelist if I didn't change.

Swallowing hard, I realized that I had to assume the responsibility as head of my household and become desperate to change my ways. I had to will that I loved my wife. So, I started getting up every morning and saying: "Today, I will to love my wife. I will nurture and cherish her today." Simultaneously, I quit nursing grudges and building walls. I began to appreciate Dana. Instead of focusing on her shortcomings, I saw her great value and worth as a person and a godly woman.

Another lesson I learned through this gut-checking time was that I didn't have the right to silence her because she got on my nerves or because I mistakenly thought she was nagging me. I saw that God was frustrating my prayers because of it. First Peter 3:7 puts it clearly, "You husbands likewise, live with your wives in an understanding way, as with a weaker vessel, since she is a woman; and grant her honor as a fellow heir of the grace of life, so that your prayers may not be hindered."

Men, did you catch the significance of that verse? If you don't love and honor your wife, then God will deal with you. You have a choice to make. You can appreciate your wife, meaning you are to be sensitively aware of her value. Or depreciate her by cheapening and belittling her. In marriage, love is a policy, not an emotion.

*Responsibility #2: Watch out for the little bugs.*

As the head of your family, you must assume responsibility for maintaining peace in your home. The following parable says it best: "A mighty tree stood high upon a mountain. It survived the hail, the heavy snow, the storms, the bitter cold of many years. Then finally it was felled by an attack of little beetles. And so it is with marriage."[5]

Anger, bitterness, grudges, and resentment breed disunity in home life. These little bugs gnaw away at the fabric of marriage, ruining your commitment and mutual respect. You must strive to secure peace in your home at all costs, because the little bugs eat their way to huge fault lines.

A good rule of thumb appears in Ephesians 4:26–27: "Be angry, and yet do not sin; do not let the sun go down on your anger, and do not give the devil an opportunity." The word *opportunity* means "a place." Don't let the devil, through anger, get a toehold in your marital or family relationships. I can't count the number of times Dana and I have stayed up past midnight resolving our differences. We are glad we labored through these difficulties (marriage is hard work) so we could achieve unity. We never would have made it, though, without a commitment to seek God's best for our marriage.

Fathers, you also have an obligation to set the tone for your children. How you treat their mother determines how they react to her. Never let your children see you arguing or fighting with your wife. That doesn't mean just do it behind closed doors. But you need to air your differences calmly and in private. Otherwise, you discredit your authority because of the division your children see. They will grow up with dysfunctional attitudes, and eventually treat their mates the same way.

In addition, if you can't live in harmony and show Christian love for your mate, your children will likely reject God and will feel that your faith is worthless. A father must set the example by honoring and praising his wife, publicly and in front of his children. This will reinforce respect and bring peace to your home.

*Responsibility #3: You must discipline your children.*

The sheriff's office in a Texas city once distributed a list of rules titled, *How to Raise a Juvenile Delinquent in Your Family*: "Begin with infancy to give the child everything he wants. This will insure his believing that the world owes him a living. Pick up everything he leaves lying around. This will teach him he can always throw off responsibility on others. Take his part against neighbors, teachers, policemen; they are all prejudiced against your child. He is a 'free spirit' and never wrong. Finally, prepare yourself for a life of grief. You're going to have it."[6]

There are biblical guidelines here as well. In Hebrews 12:5–8, the writer is speaking primarily of spiritual sons, but this can be applied to natural sons: "And you have forgotten the exhortation which is addressed to you as sons, 'My son, do not regard lightly the discipline of the Lord, nor faint when you are reproved by Him; for those whom the Lord loves He disciplines, and He scourges every son whom He receives.' It is for discipline that you endure; God deals with you as with sons; for what son is there whom his father does not discipline? But if you are without discipline, of which all have become partakers, then you are illegitimate children and not sons." Verse 11 adds, "All discipline for the moment seems not to be joyful, but sorrowful; yet to those who have been trained by it, afterwards it yields the peaceful fruit of righteousness."

The Old Testament priest, Eli, is an example of a father who didn't discipline his sons and reaped disaster. You can read his story in 1 Samuel, chapters 2 through 4. 1 Samuel 3:13 sums it up, when the Lord tells Samuel, "For I have told him that I am about to judge his house forever for the iniquity which he knew, because his sons brought a curse on themselves and he did not rebuke them."

Disciplining children doesn't simply mean swinging a paddle in their direction when they misbehave. That is often the easy way out. Discipline requires education, training, instructing, and nurturing—and, when necessary, rebuking. This is "tough" love; tough because it hurts to administer discipline on your children, but absolutely necessary for proper training.

Proverbs 13:24 says, "He who spares the rod *hates his son,* But he who loves him disciplines him diligently" (italics added). If this verse is true, my parents loved me a lot! Sadly, I see too many modern fathers who must hate their children, because they pamper them and never correct their bad habits. Yes, it is tough setting guidelines and refusing to tolerate childish rebellion and manipulation. But it pays off when they grow up into courteous, well-mannered adults.

Power Team member Keith Davis told me once about his son's disobedience. He announced to Josiah that he had done wrong, which meant discipline. With all the innocence a three-year-old could muster, he said seriously, "Daddy, Jesus wouldn't spank the children." Keith said he couldn't stop laughing. Still, because his father disciplines him, Josiah is one of the most secure, well-mannered little boys I've ever known.

I've had similar times with our oldest son, Stephen. In one of his "terrible two" modes, he picked up a cherry tomato at dinner and prepared to launch it across the room. Looking at him sternly, I said, "Son, you throw that and you're getting a spanking." Glaring back at me, this pint-sized lad made his best Clint Eastwood face and said, "Go ahead, make my day." So I did! He is a strong-willed boy, and, without discipline, would literally run the family. Proverbs 22:6 says, "Train up a child in the way he should go, even when he is old he will not depart from it." Dads, dare to teach your children and rest on God's grace.

*Responsibility #4: Get on your knees and fight like a man.*

Real men cover their families spiritually. They are men of principle and biblical convictions. They set the example through constant prayer, privately and with their families, and by leading family devotions in God's Word. They are known as pillars in their local church. Not as rulers in high positions, but because they faithfully attend, serve, and support their pastor.

Real men don't grumble constantly. Because of their strong faith, they stand on God's promises and know that He will supply their provisions according to His riches in glory (Phil. 4:19). They also wear the full armor of God, as outlined in Ephesians 6:11–17 and will "with all prayer and petition pray at all times in the Spirit, and with this in view, be on the alert with all perseverance and petition for all the saints" (verse 18). They will, as the apostle Paul counseled the men of his time, "Be on the alert, stand firm in the faith, act like men, be strong" (1 Cor. 16:13).

*Responsibility #5: Take financial responsibility.*

Earlier in this chapter I noted 1 Timothy 5:8, which says a man who will not provide for his family is worse than an unbeliever. Paul is equally blunt in 2 Thessalonians 3:10, "For even when we were with you, we used to give you this order: if anyone will not work, neither let him eat."

To start a family without any financial plan is immature and irresponsible. When it comes to setting a dark mood within a family, financial pressure is the king. If you aren't careful and don't properly manage your income (through faith and by not living beyond your means), it can crush you. Wise men will establish a budget and seek financial counsel. This will provide a buffer zone and bring tranquility to your home.

A word of caution here: Balance is the key to life. While you must provide for your family, don't take it to extremes. Workaholics often neglect their children. Childhood only comes once. Don't miss one of the greatest joys you will ever know, spending time with your children and watching them grow into mature men and women.

## Conclusion

As men, we are accountable for the kind of person, husband, and father we have made of ourselves. As William Bennett notes in *The Book of Virtues:* "That's just the way I am! is not an excuse for inconsiderate or vile behavior. Nor is it even an accurate description, for we are never just what we are. As Aristotle was among the first to insist, we become what we are as persons by the decisions that we ourselves make."[7]

Family is the cornerstone of a civilized nation. We need godly men who will lead their families, and in so doing, impact our nation and world for the glory of God. To do great things, though, you must first have control of yourself. Read the next chapter for tips on battling your number one enemy: lust.

### Gut Check

1. What are some of your romantic images of marriage? Are they realistic?

2. What does marriage mean to you? Is it a never-ending commitment? Why? (See Prov. 5:18–19, Matt. 19:5–6, and 1 Cor. 7:3–9.)

3. What are the responsibilities you must meet as part of marriage? (See Eph. 5:22–33, 1 Pet. 3:7 and 1 Tim. 5:8. Also, although 1 Tim. 3:1–5 speaks to overseers, or bishops, these are good guidelines for any man.)

4. If you are married:

a. Write down a description of the state of your marriage. Ask your mate to do the same.

b. Compare notes with your mate.

c. List ways you can improve your marriage. For example, if you struggle to communicate, set aside one night a week as a "date night" where you have undistracted devotion to each other. Or set aside thirty minutes alone (no TV, kids or phone calls) where you can talk with your wife. This is vital for ministering to a woman's unique needs.

5. If you are single:

a. Write a short essay of what you are looking for in a marital partner.

b. What type of man will you need to be in order to be worthy of such a relationship?

Power Team founder John Jacobs smashing several hundred pounds of ice while Tom is sandwiched between two thousand nails

USC Coach John Robinson and Tom share a moment prior to a game.

Open-air preaching to university students in Manila

A. C. Green celebrates another World
Championship ring with the L. A. Lakers

Heavy weight champion Earnie Shavers, Hall of Fame for Most Fights Won by TKO, demonstrates his style for University of Arizona football team.

Former USC Coach Larry Smith receives CFC
Award of Courage

Bret Holman sharing his testimony at USC

Taking A. C. Green to the hoop. Of course, the four-step ladder helped!

Baptism at A. I. M. Conference

Power feat—forearm strike

Tom inflating a
hot water bottle

Wedding Day for Tom and Dana

Keith Davis preaches at Lawton, Oklahoma, army base

John Jacobs preaches to young people

Smashing several hundred pounds of ice while under two thousand nails

Power Team founder
John Jacobs bending
a steel bar

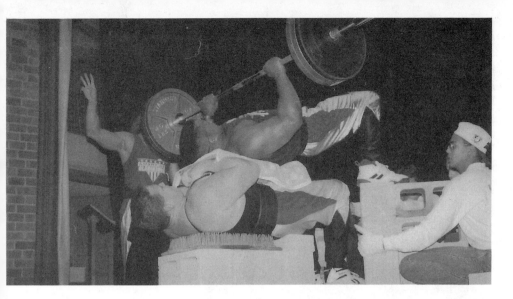

Keith Davis bench pressing 315 pounds while Tom is sandwiched between two thousand nails

Keith Davis and Tom doing the double arm sandwich

Tom snapping
handcuffs.
Power Team
founder John Jacobs
watches

Team Prayer,
USC Rose Bowl

# 9

## BATTLING LUST

*Guys see sex as a sport. . . . Everything to them is winning and losing. They don't like losing and in their minds if they're not having sex with their girlfriends, they're losing.*

—*Seventeen-year-old girl*
*from McComb, Mississippi*[1]

FORMER NEW YORK GIANTS' PLAYER and Power Team member Keith Davis tells an amusing, though very sad, story. As he and the guys pulled away from a high school parking lot after an appearance, a girl came running after their van. Frantically waving her hands, she screamed hysterically: "Power Team! Wait!" Seeing she was sobbing uncontrollably, Davis asked, "What's wrong?"

"It's . . . it's . . . my boy-oy-oy-friend," she stuttered.

"Did he hit you? Abuse you? What happened?" Davis asked with deep concern.

"No-o-o-o-o . . . " she sniveled. "It's much worse than that. He said he was go-o-o-o-ing to break up with me . . . " Pausing as she tried to stop sobbing, she finally continued, "He said if I didn't lose ten pounds, he was going to break up with me."

"Hey, you want to get rid of 150 pounds?" Keith responded. "Dump your boyfriend. Find someone who cares for you for who you are, not how you look."

There is a huge difference in a man loving a girl or just lusting after her attractive, slender body. True satisfaction can only come from a relationship founded upon God's principles and built in a spirit of purity. Trying to find love and security through a succession of sex partners is like looking for a bar of gold in a pile of manure.

The Bible warns continually against lust in all forms. James 1:15 calls it the first step toward sin, which brings death. Second Peter 1:4 blames it for the corruption in the world, while 1 John 2:16 says the lust of the flesh and eyes, and the pride of life, is not of the Father. Galatians 5:16 advises you to walk in the Spirit so that you won't want to fulfill fleshly lusts.

While lust is more than sexual arousal, that is a crucial problem for many men. The Bible is clear on this issue. Proverbs 6:25 tells us not to lust after strange women. In Matthew 5:28, Jesus equates lusting after a woman in your heart with committing adultery.

Where do you stand in the battle against lust?

- If you're a young, single male, it is easy to feel lonely and crave intimacy with the opposite sex. Yet, you must wait patiently for the Lord to bring you into that close relationship you want. As I said throughout the last two chapters, it won't be easy. But it will be worth it. Nor is it an impossible battle. If it was easy, everybody would do it. But there's a price to pay if you want God's best.

- If you're married, you already know that walking to the altar didn't kill those fleshly desires and stuff them face down in the church pew. Of course, the world says, "Looking never hurts." When looking leads to more, it burns. Proverbs 6:27 says, "Can a man take fire in his bosom, and his clothes not be burned?" So, married men, don't let lust master you and make you do things you will regret.

### Helpful Hints

Single or married, lust is a lifelong battle. Here are some helpful hints for fighting it.

- Make sure you have a strong foundation in God's Word. This will help you spiritually, morally, ethically, and in your daily habits. "How can a young man keep his way pure? By keeping it according to Thy Word" (Ps. 119:9).

- Find your destiny in God and set a direction for your life. This is a key to finding the Lord's blessing, occupationally and personally. If you're single, He won't join you with someone who doesn't share your calling and vision. The two of you will be compatible, because God already knows both of your hearts. Married men, you will find greater unity with your mate as God matures you. Marriage is the uniting of two people to share life spiritually and physically.

- Become financially secure. There is rarely a financially "perfect" time for marriage, starting a family, and so forth. But do you have a plan? Do you tithe from your income (including part-time work) to the Lord's work? Do you have a budget and carefully manage your money? Or do you blow so much on movies, ball games, pizza, clothes, and credit card bills that there's more money than month? The time to make financial plans is when you're young. You build foundations today for your future responsibilities—and they are serious.

- Single men, if the pursuit of lovely women or relationships dominates your thoughts, place this idol before Christ. In your mind, hang it on the cross, pray that you will die to it, and ask God to purify the desires of your heart.

Many of you healthy, red-blooded men will say: "Tom, I want to trust God in my sex life. I want to walk pure and holy. But I'm struggling with lust." Well, congratulations. You're a normal man. Remember what I said: Lust is a master passion. God created us with a strong sex drive to perpetuate the human race and as an incentive to keep families together.

Ever since Adam and Eve sinned, Satan has been trying to pervert that force and trick humans into misusing it. In the past thirty years, he has succeeded, deceiving millions into thinking they are finding freedom and satisfaction. Actually, the list of rewards from the "sexual revolution" includes things like rape, child abuse, rampant divorce, and so much suspicion and disunity that our country's social fabric is unraveling.

I continually talk with brothers, single and married, who battle lust. They struggle with things like masturbation, unclean thoughts, or fighting the passion stirred up by sexy TV shows or movies (they need to close their eyes and quit watching).

Archibald Hart, dean of the Graduate School of Psychology at Fuller Theological Seminary, surveyed six hundred married men (mostly Christians) recently. His findings support my personal observations. Of these so-called "good" married men:

° Sixty-one percent struggle with masturbation.

° Ninety-one percent of those from Christian homes reported exposure to pornography within two years of puberty, and 71 percent said it was destructive to their sexuality.

° Fifty-nine percent fantasize about having sex with someone other than their wife. [2]

Yet, the misery you experience from following through on lustful thoughts fades in comparison to the ensuing guilt and condemnation. Now, listen carefully. I am not giving you an excuse to sin. Still, if you fall, at least fall forward. Get up and run to God, not away from Him.

Naturally, when you stumble and sin, the last place you want to go is before the Lord and confess it. But Proverbs 24:16 says, "For a righteous man falls seven times, and rises again, but the wicked stumble in time of calamity." Even righteous, dedicated believers in Christ make mistakes. Look at King David's heart. Recite his prayer of confession in Psalm 51 and then move on. Don't look back. Wallowing in guilt only keeps your mind focused on the sin. (See Ps. 31:1–7.)

## More Tips

Here are a few other tips for dealing with lust.

- Take time to study 1 Corinthians 6:9–20. Verse 16 highlights what takes place when you engage in sex: "The two will become one flesh." If you have experienced sexual encounters or deep emotional ties in the past, it may be holding you back. You can't walk free in the power of the Holy Spirit.

Because two become one in the act of sex, your spirit became enmeshed with each woman you knew intimately. Soul ties will enslave you to desires, memories, and compulsive behavior that you detest. These habits bother you, and will keep a grip on you. No matter how powerful they may appear, they can be broken. Speak the prayer below, right now:

"Lord Jesus, I fall out of agreement with *(fill in the girl's name)* and my soul tie, where we became one flesh. I withdraw my deposit and commitment to her. I ask that You would restore me to a spirit of virginity from this day forward. Thank You, Lord, that I am free by the virtue of Your blood. Amen."

Take this step for each girl you have known intimately. What if you can't remember all their names? Confess that to the Lord and ask Him to remove each tie.

- Seek deliverance to help you break free of lust. This may be necessary if you find yourself constantly harassed and unable to break these chains. Even if you have been born again and your spirit renewed, you still live in a contaminated body (the flesh). Sometimes a spirit of lust hides until a weak moment, then raises its ugly head.

Share your struggle with a mature Christian, such as your pastor or someone who has discipled you. Ask that person to pray that the oppressive spirit and root of lust would be broken and leave. As a man, you may never be completely free from attacks. But don't allow it constantly to bubble up from within.

You can deal with it more effectively by taking aggressive steps to overcome the problem. That is where Bible study is such a key. Pray as the psalmist did in Psalm 119:133, "Establish my footsteps in Thy word, and do not let any iniquity have dominion over me." And, remember the words of Psalm 119:9: "How can a young man keep his way pure? By keeping it according to Thy word."

This war between flesh and spirit is furious. Paul reviews it in Romans 7–8. Chapter 7, verse 15 describes it in detail, "For that which I am doing, I do not understand; for I am not practicing what I would like to do, but I am doing the very thing I hate." Your flesh diametrically opposes your Christian spirit. With this battle going on, the one you feed (spirit or flesh) determines whether you will live in victory or constantly struggle with defeat.

- A tactic I still use when I'm traveling and am away from my wife is to ask the Lord to put my sexual desires to sleep until the appropriate time. Not only does this help stem the tides that can spring up easily within me, but it also increases the satisfaction from marital intimacy.

- Single men, pray for God's perfect choice for your mate. Begin to cover her in prayer. Stand on the promises of God's Word. Here are a few. Write them down. Confess them aloud. Tape them on the wall.

–Psalm 37:4–5; 7, 23: "Delight yourself in the Lord; and He will give you the desires of your heart. Commit your way to the Lord, trust also in Him, and He will do it. Rest in the Lord and wait patiently for Him. The steps of a man are established by the Lord; and He delights in his way."

–Proverbs 18:22: "He who finds a wife finds a good thing, and obtains favor from the Lord."

–Psalm 84:11: "For the Lord God is a sun and shield; the Lord gives grace and glory; No good thing does He withhold from those who walk uprightly."

–Proverbs 19:14: "House and wealth are an inheritance from fathers, but a prudent wife is from the Lord."

The spouse God has for you will be an incredible blessing. But you've got to search for her in God's way. Married men already know marriage is the closest thing on earth to heaven—or hell—you will ever know. Trust Jesus, wait for the Lord's selection, and it will be joyful. There is only one girl God created for you, and He is great enough to bring her your way. In His time, not yours. Since you can't speed it up or slow it down, *stop worrying!*

Married men, the above section applies to you, too. Your wife needs the covering of your daily prayers. You, too, need to pray for her continued spiritual growth and God's favor over her. What if you're struggling with the choice you've already made? You already know that marriage is hard work and a lifetime of adjustment. The answer, though, won't come from walking away. Prayer can help you and your wife turn your marriage back into the romantic relationship of the past.

### Sexual Games

You may be asking: "So what? Most guys are out doing it and they're okay. Why should I wait? Why should I even worry about controlling my lust? Who else does?" Yes, it seems that way in the permissive 1990s. American colleges and universities used to quibble over whether to allow men to visit a woman's dorm (and vice versa). Now, many stage things like "National Condom Week" or games of "Pin the Condom on Elvis." It is insane. And wrong.

Many college guys say: "Hey, man, if you love a girl, why not? Hey, I can't expect to marry a girl if we're not compatible." Right. What a lame excuse. I know guys who are running around trying to find out if they're compatible with twenty-five or thirty women a year. And trying to justify this reckless behavior by calling it love.

First Corinthians 13:4–8 spells out what love really is: "Love is patient, love is kind, and is not jealous; love does not brag and is not arrogant, does not act unbecomingly; it does not seek its own, is not provoked, does not take into account a wrong suffered, does not rejoice in unrighteousness, but rejoices with the truth; bears all things, believes all things, hopes all things, endures all things. Love never fails."

Above all else, love is patient. As the popular abstinence campaign says, "True love waits." It doesn't push, like guys who say, "If you really love me, you'll have sex with me." Wise females hearing that garbage will respond, "If you really love and respect me, you'll have the guts to wait until marriage."

The only problem with patience is that you may never understand its rewards until you reach the two primary goals: marriage with your virginity intact, and sexual fulfillment solely through your lifetime partner. I have yet to hear anyone say they are sorry they waited until marriage to have sex, and a 1994 survey by the Sex Information and Education Council of the United States (SIECUS) backs that up. They found that, of the teens who had had sex, half wished they had delayed the experience.[4] Yet there are countless stories of emotionally bruised people, many also scarred physically from sexually-transmitted diseases, because they couldn't wait for a little fun.

Think it is always men who are eager to hop into bed? Not true. I remember a college football player who didn't want to have premarital sex. His girlfriend kept inviting, enticing, urging, and badgering until he caved in. After awhile she dumped him, complaining he was a lousy lover. He lost all self-respect, and had literally quit dating, afraid of encountering another female who might discard him like an old shoe.

This reflects many relationships on college campuses and in singles' bars. Difficult to prove, because so few will talk about it openly. Yet the victims of these messed-up relationships visit our meetings constantly, looking for answers and hoping desperately to find love. They come asking for prayer, whispering about their pain and rejection. If they refuse Christ's love, they will nurse their wounds for years. It will be tougher than carrying a 500-pound gorilla around in a backpack.

### The Virgin

Virginity has a glory that is valuable before *and after* marriage. The spirit behind virginity is a spirit of purity. If you wonder why you struggle with lust, it could be because you lost your virginity before marriage and never asked God to restore that spirit. I know. I wasted my precious gift; recovering it took countless hours of prayer and seeking godly counsel.

Again, Jesus is the best model to follow. Look at His lifestyle. Tempted in every way, He never gave in to sin. Jesus was so secure in His relationship with His Father that He didn't need a woman hanging around his neck, making Him feel secure and confirming His masculinity. He felt secure in God's love.

After years of observation, I believe the number one reason men and women get involved in immorality is not because they're sex-crazed. They are love-starved. Craving intimacy, they seek to find one who deeply loves them, cares about them, and will forever be faithful.

Hollywood plays out this fantasy through pictures of romance and love that make people think love is a bowl of perfect cherries—rosy sweetness and no pits. Not only is that a lie, so are its portrayals of out-of-wedlock sexual relationships that are always full of fun, joy, and happiness. They never show you the teenage boy dying of AIDS, who said, "The rock singers told me about sex but they never told me I'd wind up like this."[5]

That is why a relationship with Jesus is so important. His love will provide the three things today's younger generation cries out for: (1) security, (2) stability, and (3) identity. Wrap yourself in Jesus's love. Then you won't try to find a dream mate or personal fulfillment in an old, run-down bar, which, if you think about it for a minute, is a pretty ridiculous place to look.

When you know the security of a personal relationship with Christ, you will find the type of glory in virginity that will help you lead a holy, pure life. Men, not only do you need to strive for a spirit of virginity throughout your life, but also you need to support such a stand among your female friends. Believe it or not, they face the same kind of pressure you do.

During a series of talks I gave at a school in Pennsylvania, a woman came up and said: "Thank God for your message on the glory of virginity this week. I've been bombarded by my friends. They're always asking, 'Why don't you lose that virginity?' They say I need to experience life, that I shouldn't waste my best years and that I should have fun while I'm still young."

They kept the pressure up to the point where she almost gave in just to shut them up. After she heard me talk about the glory of virginity, when her buddies berated her, she snapped back: "I can have what you've got any day of the week. But you can never again have what I've got." Boom! That shut them up for good.

You may be saying: "This is too tough. I can't do that. That's just too much pressure." Well, following Christ is tough. It calls for a lifetime of commitment. Withstanding the pressure to be sexually promiscuous is only the beginning. Keep reading. You will face other challenges if you want to become one of Christ's disciples. Lots of men couldn't handle the task. You will read about them in the next chapter.

### Gut Check

1. If you are single:

a. List several advantages for abstaining from sex until marriage.

b. List the advantages of remaining faithful to your future partner. Do you know anyone whose life was shattered because of premarital sex?

c. Do you habitually struggle with lust, pornography, or impure desires? How can reading the Bible each day help you control those habits?

d. How does lust affect your relationship with God?

2. Whether you are single or married, do you believe you can have victory over lustful desires and live a pure life? Look up 1 Corinthians 10:13; Hebrews 4:15–16; 1 Peter 2:11; and 2 Peter 2:9. Write them down, pray them out loud and memorize them. Follow this formula for victory over lust:

a. Pray (Matt. 26:41).

b. Spend time in the Word daily (Ps. 119:9).

c. Be ruthless with sin (Matt. 5:27–30).

d. Flee from evil desires (2 Tim. 2:22).

3. Have you had sex before marriage or committed adultery?

a. If you are single, you can never regain your physical virginity. But you can obtain forgiveness, cleansing, and the spirit of virginity by falling out of agreement with past partners. Go back to page 107 and pray the prayer listed there.

b. If you are married, you need to restore purity to your marriage. In most cases, this requires (at the right time) confession to your wife. But first consult your pastor to ask for wisdom on how to approach the subject.

4. Hundreds of thousands of young men and women across the country have signed a pledge to remain sexually pure until marriage because "True Love Waits." If you are single and agree with this stand, write out your commitment to abstain from sex until marriage. Sign it in front of witnesses such as your parents, pastor, and close Christian friends.

# 10

## THE THREE AMIGOS

*Live in such a way that you would not be ashamed to sell your parrot to the town gossip.*

—*Will Rogers*[1]

H EY, C'MON! LET'S HAVE FUN!" yell the party animals. "Get drunk. Get crazy. Get some women. Live it up, dudes! Hey, you Christians. Narrow-minded. Dull. B-o-o-o-o-r-r-r-r-ing." Right. Guys like that wind up with hangovers, die in car wrecks, need treatment for sexually transmitted diseases, or get AIDS. Still want to have "fun"?

Unfortunately, many Christians do. Not so blatantly. But with one foot in church, they still want to dip a few toes in the world. If you feel that way, why bother? No sense pretending. You won't feel any less hung over in the morning, or any better when you face your friends. At least you won't lead others astray by playing church but living like the devil the rest of the week.

Ironically, it's not Christianity that makes some people think this life is boring. It's "religiosity," people acting pious and friendly at church while living a different way outside the walls. Authentic Christian relationships provide fellowship, unity, and camaraderie that can't be matched by the world. The selflessness of Christian love is far superior to the selfish, self-serving, self-seeking fun worshiped by the world.

This Christian brotherhood is necessary for maintaining a close walk with God. It helps strengthen you to be the kind of man Jesus wants, those fully under His lordship, who will lay down their lives for His kingdom. As He taught His disciples in Matthew 6:10, "Thy kingdom come. Thy will be done, on earth as it is in heaven." That means you won't quit, no matter what you think will happen, for as long as you breathe.

In the 1990s, many Christians are looking for Christ's return. They shrug and say: "Why bother trying to change anything? The world's going down the tubes anyway. Let's just hang on until Jesus comes back." Ever hear that old line about history repeating itself? This is exactly what people were saying in the 1930s. A belief circulated that Jesus *had* to be coming back. Its supporters urged, "Don't go to college or get married, Jesus will return." Instead, Hitler came and touched off World War II. The misguided belief that the world wouldn't last past 1940 stripped a generation of the preparation to fulfill its destiny.

Simply lying down and waiting for Jesus is a tragedy when the world is dying for answers. Oh, we believe we're a "religious" nation. Various polls show 80 to 90 percent of Americans claiming born-again status. What a joke. If those figures were true, our nation wouldn't suffer the plagues of crime, divorce, drug abuse, pornography, sexual abuse, and social and urban decay.

That is why Jesus needs disciples—men committed to follow Him regardless of the price, who will stand for right in the face of criticism and ridicule, who will be faithful church members where they will be held accountable by close brothers and mature in their faith. If this was easy, there wouldn't be a shortage of disciples.

The Bible illustrates the kind of followers who lived in Jesus's day, good and bad. Not surprisingly, they're similar to today's crowd. You can find them in Luke 9:57–62 and Isaiah 6:1–8. Luke shows the three disciples I call, "The Three Amigos." Sound like a gang of cartoon characters? They are pretty goofy.

## The Rash Disciple

Luke 9:57–58 gives the first example: "And as they were going along the road, someone said to Him, 'I will follow You wherever You go.' And Jesus said to him, 'The foxes have holes, and the birds of the air have nests, but the Son of Man has nowhere to lay His head.'"

This enthusiastic bragger is an example of the rash (or heedless) disciple. He's an airhead. Headstrong and reckless, overcome by impulse, such men are quick to promise the moon and slow to ride the rocket. They don't consider their commitments. I can imagine guys back then grinning: "Hey, this sounds great. Let's go! Jesus. What a trip. You hear about the time He told Peter to go fishing? Caught one with gold in its mouth, man. He feeds thousands. Heals people. Even raises the dead. Yeah, man, Jesus is cool."

As long as Christ did exciting miracles and everything went smoothly, crowds followed. When He sought total commitment, most walked away. Finally, He asked the last twelve disciples, "Are you going to leave too?" You need to understand that Jesus wasn't pleading with them to stay. He was saying, in effect, "I'll lay out the commitment and you can either be My disciple or leave. Don't make a rash decision."

Momentary excitement lured the disciple in Luke 9:57–58. Jesus' preaching charmed this man and he swelled with enthusiasm. He was ready to follow the Lord anywhere. But you can't last long on emotion. So Jesus poses a question that implies, "Look, will you really follow Me? Do you understand what you're pledging, where this path leads? Let me spell it out. You won't have any downy soft pillows. No microwave ovens. No home. This could cost you your reputation or your life. Look, this is tough. No momma or daddy to fall back on, no worldly safety or security. If you're going to follow Me, let's make sure you trust God."

Following Him means living by faith. Total reliance and dependence on God. It sounds easy. But living it is a different matter. Jesus said in Luke 14:27, "Whoever does not carry his own cross and come after Me cannot be My disciple." The message hasn't changed. Count the cost before claiming you want to be His disciple.

How often have you heard others make rash boasts about their faithfulness? I remember a student at San Jose State University who came to one of our ministry meetings. At first he was smiling and full of enthusiasm. Everyone thought he must be a solid believer. Afterward, we talked for awhile. He admitted he wasn't living a clean lifestyle and said: "I want to repent and commit my life to the Lord. I know what I'm doing is wrong." But as soon as I talked about the need for commitment, he mumbled some gibberish, turned around, and walked away.

One problem with Christianity is that the public sees us as money-grubbing hypocrites. They reject Jesus and the church because of compromising, lukewarm, backslidden believers. Countless numbers of counterfeit converts have made decisions for Christ, but never became His disciples. They come to Jesus with a weak foundation and fail to complete the work. They fall away from church, mess around with the world, and ultimately slip back into gross immorality. No wonder the world mocks them.

In Matthew 13:20–21, Jesus talks about life's rocky soil. He's drawing a parallel to the persecution and affliction all Christians will face. Those without solid roots in God's Word, determined to live His way, will give up. It takes commitment to withstand life's trials and pressures.

College students are especially prone to following the crowd. They get around a Christian group and say, "I know this is how I should be." Then when they go back to their athletic teams, fraternities, or friendly cliques, their courage fades at the first hint of criticism. If you can't face that kind of pressure, what will you do when real oppression comes? When they throw Christians in jail for protesting abortion or the state padlocks your church, what will you do? Since it doesn't attract much press coverage, you may not have noticed: *those things are already happening.*

I know a young international student at USC. One of her professors tried to bully her into writing an article favoring abortion. If she refused, she would forget her high grade in the class. With tears streaming down her face, she stood strong for what she believed.

When persecution like that becomes widespread, will you pay the price to declare you're a Christian? Are you willing to sit in jail for a few days or a few years for the gospel? Philippians 3:8 says we need to count everything we have as rubbish for the sake of Christ. That is a cause that takes deep commitment, not a rash decision.

### The Procrastinator

Luke 9:59–60 shows the second of "The Three Amigos": "And He said to another, 'Follow Me.' But he said, 'Permit me first to go and bury my father.' But He said to him, 'Allow the dead to bury their own dead; but as for you, go and proclaim everywhere the kingdom of God.'"

This guy wasn't a volunteer like the first amigo. No, Jesus called him to preach the gospel full time. His excuse shows how his concern for the world kept him from obedience. He searched for a reason to put it off a little longer. His father hadn't really died. Otherwise, he would have been home grieving. Jesus would have said: "That's good, son. Catch up with us later."

No, it is more likely Dad was a little sick, and he was waiting around for him to die. That could take years. He had made it his duty to stay and watch, but Jesus was saying: "You're entangled with your family. I have a higher duty for you. I need you to go preach the gospel."

He was telling this man that God's kingdom suffers from neglect and needs help. Few are spiritually alive, and even fewer are qualified to preach and teach. Since he was capable and spiritually alive, Jesus told him to leave his father's care to those who were spiritually dead and couldn't answer His call. But he was a procrastinator. This man fell prey to one of the most dangerous words in the English vocabulary—*tomorrow*. Bur for too many , tomorrow never comes or they just plain run out of tomorrows. All the tomorrows become "too lates." Such people still run amok today, saying things like:

- God, there's this little problem. It's this crummy town I was raised in, the people around here. I just need to move to the West Coast so I can be free. Then I'll serve You.

- I've got some financial problems right now. My credit card balance is so high. I need to work Sundays to pay off these bills. As soon as I do that, Lord, I'll serve You.

- God, I'm in the prime of life. I'm young. I need my education. I've got to study. Practice football. With all this stuff goin' on,

I don't have any time left for church. But when I've got my degree, I'll serve You.

- I'm going to try to be a businessman; if that doesn't work out, then I'll go into ministry. Or, I'm going to try law school and be a lawyer first. Then I'll have my education, and I can always fall back on ministry.

Such folks have it all wrong. If you're not serving God now, right where you are, you won't make a dramatic change overnight. When you finish one task, you will find another one waiting ... for the rest of your life. That is how a man who intends to serve God at 21, but procrastinates, will reach 75 and never do it. There will be marriage, children, jobs, promotions, vacations, weddings, funerals, graduations, grandchildren ... and finally, his funeral.

Nor is being a minister of the gospel something to fall back on if nothing else works out. It's your number one priority, regardless of how you earn a living. Businessman, doctor, lawyer, professional athlete, or ditch digger, you are a missionary to your profession. That takes a full-time commitment. Don't waste years trying stupid alternatives before you see the light.

Nothing should stop you from fulfilling God's call. Your obligation is to please Him ... period. When I preach this, people ask, "God is concerned about my pleasure and happiness, isn't He?" Not nearly as much as He cares about your obedience and worship. Offer obedience and worship to God, and the pleasures will come. Psalms 16:11 says, "In Thy presence is fulness of joy; in Thy right hand there are pleasures forever."

### Double-Minded Disciple

The third disciple portrayed in Luke 9 wavers in his commitment. Verses 61–62: "And another also said, 'I will follow You, Lord; but first permit me to say good-bye to those at home.' But Jesus said to him, 'No one, after putting his hand to the plow and looking back, is fit for the kingdom of God.'"

This man is straddling the fence, pulled between serving God and himself. Not that it was wrong to say farewell to his family, but once he went back home, he probably would never leave. It would be too much fun, too comfortable. He would regret leaving his loved ones behind, and he would think it over until he forgot his commitment.

Double-mindedness and compromises cause people to fall into sin. James 1:8 says the double-minded man is unstable in all his ways. Do you ever see people coming to the altar to accept Jesus as their Savior—or rededicate their lives to Him—six, eight or ten times? Their heart is half in God's kingdom and half in the world. The flesh inevitably overcomes the spirit.

Like this third amigo, I see many who won't make a break with the world. People who say: "I've got this girlfriend (or boyfriend) and she's (or he's) not saved. But I really love this person and I want to stay with her or him to be a witness." Who would be so cruel as to tell someone to break up with a girlfriend? The Lord! Second Corinthians 6:17 says, "Come out from their midst and be separate," while verse 14 counsels, "Do not be bound together with unbelievers; for what partnership have righteousness and lawlessness, or what fellowship has light with darkness?"

God tells believers throughout the Bible not to fellowship with the world. Fellowship means an exchange, where you draw life from another person. What does the world offer? Lust, greed, pride, drunkenness, sexual promiscuity and every negative thing you can dream of (read Gal. 5:19–21).

In other words, don't go to their parties and drink their booze, smoke their dope, or sniff their cocaine so you can be a good buddy. Yes, you can witness to unsaved people and be a friend. Give them what you have, though, don't seek out what they have. God wants you to live as a light to the world. Speak kindly. Offer your help. Be a friend when the fair-weather friends split. Show others you're different.

Jesus said in Luke 9:62 that we shouldn't put our hand to the plow and look back. He means don't crave the world in your heart. That itch will overcome the best of intentions; jealousy, lust, and envy can't be buried forever.

Instead, focus your aim. A plow illustrates perfectly the devotion that it takes to follow God. Plowing a field demands concentration. To plow straight rows, a farmer must watch straight ahead. One glance back, one distraction, and the whole thing goes off track. And so it is with your life as a disciple.

Double-mindedness is a serious flaw. It prevents many from answering God's call on their life. I have known young men in their twenties who struggle with His call for years. They hear God's call, but never mature spiritually. They allow the lure of making money to draw them away from serving God.

Others stumble because of their families. Some parents have yelled crazy things like, "I'd rather have my son smoking dope and drinking than hanging around you Christians!" Or they will tell their sons: "Well, I think you're getting a little carried away. You're in a cult. They just want your money."

That happened with one man who used to be one of the biggest cocaine dealers at USC. One morning he woke up scared to death, terrified that somebody was out to get him. He accepted Jesus as his Savior, cleaned up his life, and made a miraculous turnaround. Then his parents convinced him he was "too fanatical." The peer pressure intensified because of that, he dropped out of sight and back into sin. During the next three years, his alcohol abuse caused five car wrecks. Thankfully, he came back to God. Still, he paid a terrible price for caving in to pressure.

Matthew 10:37–38 says, "He who loves father or mother more than Me is not worthy of Me; and he who loves son or daughter more than Me is not worthy of Me. And he who does not take his cross and follow after Me is not worthy of Me." The Lord is saying that your love for Him should take first place in your heart, even above your parents or children. You won't know that kind of love if you try to follow the world and Him at the same time.

## Fully for God

This chapter wouldn't be complete without a look at a fourth disciple, the godly kind. This one comes from the Old Testament. Isaiah 6:1–8 tells of Isaiah, a very righteous man. Study this passage and you see desire for God burning in his heart. He sees angels singing, "Holy, Holy, Holy," and comes face to face with the righteous Lord. Shaken to his toes, he quivers, "Woe is me, for I am ruined!" Thankfully, an angel touched his lips with a coal (which signifies the Holy Spirit) and declared Isaiah was forgiven.

The point is that no amount of good works can get you into heaven. Lighting candles won't do it. Confessing your sins will make you feel better, but won't make you any more righteous in God's sight. You can pray until you're blue in the face, do a dozen good deeds a day, feed the poor, visit nursing homes, care for AIDS patients . . . and you will still fall short. You must turn away from your wrongs.

Repentance, though, is just the beginning. The heart of the disciple cries out, like Isaiah in verse 8, "Here am I. Send me." That need echoes across today's world. God wants those who will pledge: "Use me to go heal the sick, preach to a dying generation, and stand in the midst of corruption and wickedness as a light. Give me Your grace, God, and I'll bring grace to many." He needs those who promise: "I'll do whatever You want me to do. I'll go wherever You want me to go. My life is not mine. Your will matters the most to me."

There are three qualities that shine in Isaiah. They're the same ones you need.

1. He had strong, burning convictions for the Lord. He wouldn't back down. Strong convictions lead to great actions. You must know what you believe. Not because I said it, or a ministry requires it, or your pastor teaches it. *You have to know it is right in your heart.* Most Christians are waiting for a minister or other leader to tell them what to do. They never develop personal convictions. And they never take personal responsibility to act.

2. Isaiah had a burning vision of God's purpose for him on earth: namely, to see His kingdom established. This same spiritual insight drove Joshua, the warrior who led Israel into the promised land. In Joshua, chapter 1, God tells Joshua three times to be strong and courageous. What is your destiny on earth? While it takes strength and courage to reach it, vision will keep your eyes on the goal.

3. He had a deep hunger for the Word of God. Without this, you might as well forget the first two qualities. When Jesus told His disciples they must eat His flesh and drink His blood, He was stressing total commitment. They had to "eat" His Word—read it, study it, meditate on it, memorize it, and tell others about it—with the same devotion you use on a Big Mac. Jesus said, "If you love Me, you will keep this Word."

Imagine you had an appointment with the president of the United States. You would be there on time. (I would show up an hour early.) You need the same anticipation to meet God in His Word. Isaiah had strength because he lived to know God through His Word. If you hear God's call on your life, especially for those who have a heart for full-time ministry, don't allow entanglements, fears, or possible loss to cause you to forfeit that destiny. You serve a big God; He won't let you down. Dare to dream big and be a witness to others.

You must possess this spiritual muscle to advance in God's kingdom. Why? Because every time you move forward a tougher opponent will be waiting. That is the title of the next chapter: "New Levels, New Devils."

### Gut Check

1. What separates a disciple from a mere Christian? (See Titus 1:15–16.)

2. What is your definition of a disciple? (See Matt. 10:32–39.)

3. What does it mean to you to "take up your cross" and follow Jesus?

4. What has God called you to do as a disciple? For example, serving in your church, leading a Bible study or becoming active in a community project.

5. How can you develop strong convictions?

# *11*

## NEW LEVELS,
## NEW DEVILS

*Every step you take away from God, you will find someone*
*waiting there to tell you: "This is the right thing to do!"*

—*Pastor Phil Bonasso*
*Morning Star Ministries*

I LICKED MY LIPS AND SWALLOWED as I walked through the locker room door, trying to calm my trembling knees. One of the few football walk-ons with the perseverance to stick it out at USC, I wanted to appear ready when I reported to defensive coach Marv Goux (pronounced "goo"). He called his men "Goux's Gorillas," and bragged that they were the biggest, baddest, toughest dudes *in the nation*. He walked in and chatted with several other players before looking me straight in the eye.

"Okay, Sirotnak, I'm putting you at noseguard. You're going to learn to love to hit, or you're going to die . . . ha, ha, ha." He said it with glee in his eyes and a full-throated belly laugh that shook the room. I would have looked around to see how my teammates reacted, but I was too nervous to shift my eyes. I wouldn't forget the statement, though. He repeated it several times during the season.

It's a shame new Christians don't hear the same greeting when they accept Jesus as their Savior. Instead, they are too often welcomed to "Candyland Christian Ministry." I have heard the altar calls promising nothing but bliss: forgiveness, freedom from sin, heaven's streets of gold, and relief from hell. Yes, those are all part of the picture. But not all of it. Converts do not need sugar-coated versions of the truth, messages that life is now going to be a wonderful bed of soft, trouble-free roses. What happens when it turns out otherwise?

If all people hear are promises of the good life, the tendency for many is to accept Jesus only for what they can get. Serving Christ becomes a matter of personal benefit. The gospel should inspire us to say, "I'll serve Jesus because He's Lord and He has a right to run my life." Receiving Jesus does not wipe away your troubles. But He does promise to see you through life's challenges, and bring you out a winner.

New levels, new devils. The more you mature as a Christian, the tougher the spiritual foes you will face. Fighting them takes courage. Courage to change, to rise to new levels, to break out of mediocrity, and to accept personal responsibility for your actions. There is no better example of how far our society has strayed from God's Word than the modern fad of people blaming their problems on everyone else, like bad parents, insensitive teachers, or crummy food.

It takes guts to seek the warrior spirit, crave discipline and make personal sacrifices. Yes, this is a challenge. If you want the satisfaction and rewards that come from serving Jesus, you will not find them casually strolling down a soft path. You must be a warrior, not a wimp who whines: "It seems I've been fighting forever. How long do I have to do this?"

## Backsliders

A friend calls them "moon walkers." They once lived for Jesus Christ, but since then they have burned out. The root problem for these moon walkers (going backwards) is the same. They have lost the sense of reality that Christians are fighting a spiritual war.

In 1 Timothy 1:18–19, Paul tells Timothy that faith is like a fight. In Jeremiah 51:30 the prophet wrote, "The mighty men of Babylon have *ceased fighting.* They stay in the strongholds; Their strength is exhausted, *they are becoming like women"* (italics added). As a man, one of the most masculine, godly traits you can possess is the will to fight. This gives you the drive to achieve and conquer. Without it, you will be weak and timid.

Many Christians burn out because they lose their warlike mentality. This disposition helps you overcome ever-present obstacles in following Christ. Instead, many believers seek an absence of conflict, thinking that represents peace. No, more like Fantasy Land. Lasting peace and joy comes through obedience to God. This includes fighting adversity. As 1 Peter 1:6–7 says, "In this you greatly rejoice, even though now for a little while, if necessary, you have been distressed by various trials, that the proof [genuineness] of your faith . . . may be found to result in praise and glory and honor at the revelation of Jesus Christ."

Too many view this good fight of faith like they would basket weaving: an optional class. *It is not.* Ecclesiastes 8:8 says, "There is no discharge in the time of war." The question for the Christian is not, "Will we have to fight?" but "When?" We are at war! Either we spiritually defeat the devil, or he will overcome us.

Joshua 1:14–15 lists another reason we must keep fighting—it is not right to abandon your brothers in the midst of war. "But you shall cross before your brothers in battle array, all your valiant warriors, and shall help them, until the Lord gives your brothers rest, as He gives you, and they also possess the land which the Lord your God is giving them."

Jesus has a divine purpose for exposing us to battle. He wants to teach us the importance of the sword of the Spirit (the Word of God) and the shield of faith. He wants to create in us an unquenchable thirst to use these weapons. This is what God did when the Israelites entered the promised land. Judges 3:1–2 says, "Now these are the nations which the Lord left, *to test Israel* by them . . . only in order that the generations of the sons of Israel *might be taught war,* those who had not experienced it formerly" (italics added). In your Christian walk, you must know the value and necessity of the warlike disposition to conquer the devil.

## Climbing Mountains

As we say in the weight room, "Use it or lose it." Likewise, it is impossible to grow spiritually without added challenges. Dare to do something you've never tried before. When God starts changing your life and adjusting your attitudes, don't resist. Our spiritual philosophy should be "Change = Growth."

Early attempts to climb the world's tallest mountain illustrate the warrior attitude. In the early 1920s, an English mountain climber, George Mallory, set out to conquer Mount Everest. Putting together a climbing party, he set out. But he failed. Got a second party. Failed. For his third try in 1924, he found the best men and equipment available.

As the climbers neared the top of the mountain, an avalanche struck. Most of the party, including Mallory, died. When the survivors returned to their homeland the English authorities welcomed them with a huge banquet. As the surviving leader arose to address the audience, he looked at the framed pictures of those who died. Tears streaming down his face, he said, "I speak to you, Mount Everest, in the name of all the brave men and those yet unborn . . . you defeated us once . . . twice . . . three times. But . . . we shall some day defeat you. Because you can't get any bigger and we can."[1]

You know the end of the story. Though it took twenty-nine more years, Edmund Hillary, of New Zealand and Tenzing Norgay, a Neapalese Sherpa tribesman, finally made it to the top. Since then, many people have conquered Everest, including a United States team in 1963. The mountain never grew. But the climbers did.

What is the spiritual mountain in your life? Look unconquerable? *I guarantee you the devil won't get any bigger.* He's a weak opponent, already defeated by the power of the cross. Only you can grow bigger.

Growth is God's plan for you. The Lord is not into "progressive" education. He doesn't pass students on because it's time for the next grade. To advance in God's kingdom you must meet the challenge at hand. After each test there will be a stronger, more cunning enemy waiting.

The key to passing these tests is greeting them with joy. Whether it's financial setbacks, physical ailments, or persecution, all will strengthen you. God is on your side. You can't lose, so don't quit. If you feel like you're at the end of your rope, tie a knot in the end and hang on! And remember Romans 8:28, "And we know that God causes all things to work together for good to those who love God, to those who are called according to His purpose."

## Maturity

Because of their constant grumbling, complaining, and lack of faith, the people of Israel spent 40 years wandering in the wilderness after leaving Egypt. Yet that was not God's plan for them. Neither does He want you to remain a spiritual baby for decades.

Many spiritual infants have passed through America's churches in the last 50 years. Babes never grow, mature, or take on responsibility. Living mediocre lifestyles of compromise and sin, they avoid firm decisions and convictions. Will you rise above passive, lukewarm faith? Are you ready to embrace growth so you can face new challenges?

Once I helped counsel a young man who wanted to get engaged. John Jacobs, leader of the Power Team, and I agreed that he wasn't ready. To stress the responsibilities of marriage, I joked: "You know what? I thought I was saved until I got married."

His eyebrows raised. As you already know from chapter 8, my explanation included how I never realized how much selfishness, sorry attitudes, and bad habits I had until someone was always around to watch them—not to mention get irritated by them. Though wonderful, marriage is still a challenge, I told him. Each time I think I have made needed changes, more adjustments wait just over the horizon. As a man of God, it requires me to constantly reach new levels as a husband and father. In my walk with God, relationships with church and staff members, and living out my destiny, I will *forever* encounter more intense spiritual hurdles. I asked this young man if he was ready for the hurdle called marriage. After thinking it over, he decided to wait.

In the Bible, nobody had a better grasp of life's preparation than David. In 1 Samuel 17:32–37, the men of Israel trembled at the thought of facing the giant Goliath. But David told King Saul, "Let no man's heart fail on account of him."

How could David be so brave? After all, in those days a shepherd was the lowest of the low. But he realized God had placed him in that position (maybe he needed to learn humility), and there he talked with God. He learned outward appearances did not dictate his position. God created him to do something great. So David confidently explained to Saul that he had fought a lion and a bear to protect his flock. Both were levels to prepare him for greater tests. Goliath was next.

It didn't matter to him that he was the youngest and smallest of his brothers. (I believe that God had a plan for each of them, but they lacked the courage to tackle it.) No, God wanted to know who would pay the price to move from level one to level two to level three. David's determination made him that hero. Trusting in God to bring him the victory, he told how he fought the lion and the bear and now he would fight this Philistine. The Lord had prepared him.

Likewise, your struggles represent preparation for the future. I've heard hundreds of people moan about their setbacks. Things like:

- I've had three divorces and my life's falling apart. How can I be a witness?

- I'm a manic-depressive. How can I be an encouragement to anybody?

- I used to be in the ministry but I fell into alcoholism (or drugs or sexual perversion). There's nothing I can do now.

But through the teaching of His Word, God poses this question, "Have you ever considered that I allowed you to go through those circumstances because I'm going to raise you up to witness to others just like you?" Whatever your hardships, difficulties or shortcomings, He allowed you to go through them. Now you can minister to those who are facing the same obstacles that you survived.

## Rise Up

Decide to be like David. Don't allow Satan to push you around any longer. Don't let the devil do your thinking. Revelation 12:10 calls him "the accuser of our brethren." He not only accuses you of doing wrong, he is a master at convincing you to blame all your problems on circumstances or other people.

I realize there may be powerful reasons for feeling discouraged or defeated. Maybe you suffer from the stings of abusive parents, poverty, or growing up in a dysfunctional environment. No matter how horrible your background, the promise of Jesus is that He can lift you out of the mess. Dwelling on past hurts allows Satan to sidetrack you with wrong emotions and feelings and afflict you with a rotten self-image.

Fight you must, but not with fists, baseball bats, or guns. Second Corinthians 10:3–5 says, "For though we walk in the flesh, we do not war according to the flesh, for the weapons of our warfare are not of the flesh, but divinely powerful for the destruction of fortresses. We are destroying speculations and every lofty thing raised up against the knowledge of God, and we are taking every thought captive to the obedience of Christ."

Unfortunately, most people don't recognize the powerful potential of thoughts. Here is the natural progression of a thought. Sow a thought and you reap an act. Sow as act and you reap a habit. Sow a habit and you reap a character. Sow a character and you reap a destiny. Bad thoughts can paralyze you and dim your impact for God. You must rise above fear, failure, denial, and laziness. Do battle with these agents of darkness. To show you the importance of this, here is a sampling of wrong thinking expressed to me over the years:

- I reserve the right to say how far my commitment goes with God. I don't need anyone telling me what to do.

- Why do I need to check in with a church every week? I can have church by myself.

- Nobody's reaching out to me. My needs aren't being met.

- You're trying to control me. I'm only 22. Why should I have to live by a church's standards? They're just men's rules.

- I'm too pressured here. I need to find a church where I can be myself.

Those who make such statements wind up like Israel, wandering in a desert of frustration, disappointment, and broken dreams. They're in danger of never entering the glorious new promises God has prepared for them.

We live in a world under siege by God's spiritual enemy, Satan, and his hellish forces. If we are to enter the promised land, we must learn the art of spiritual warfare to fight on the Lord's side. That, or lay down and become the enemy's victim.

## Frustration Plus

I may sound tough. But if you're suffering setbacks, I understand. More than once I have felt like quitting. Especially when lust, temper, insecurity, or rejection overwhelmed me. Once I felt so shaken that I doubted my own salvation. When I asked my pastor why I felt that way, he said: "Tommy, I think God has given you over to the flesh in these areas (see 1 Cor. 5:5.) If you'll let the cross penetrate, God will lift you up to a new level of grace. He'll give you the ability to win over these things."

That comment hurt. But it caused me to surrender my selfishness and other bad habits. It was a key step up in waging spiritual warfare. This should be a way of life, but for most Christians it isn't. Why? They lack the heart of a warrior. Searching for spiritual pain killers, they close their eyes to the world's problems. They don't want to know about conflicts outside their peaceful little sanctuary. After all, if they know, God may hold them accountable to do something.

Others seek survival Christianity. They want to just squeak by, get their needs met, and hold on until Jesus comes to rescue them from this wicked world. Then there are those with flaky ethics, weak morality, and loose, limited commitments to God. They avoid discipline, personal sacrifice, and accountability.

Without making a decision to fight for growth and maturity, you will fall. The Bible says that as Jesus was, so are we. You must capture the warrior spirit. I don't mean to walk around in battle fatigues, carrying a gun and acting like Rambo. I'm talking about building useful character traits. When the enemy stirs up negative thoughts, it takes Christian character to resist. Without the warrior spirit, you become a wishy-washy, spineless jellyfish. With it, you will enhance your fruitfulness. I believe we will soon see history's greatest warrior: Jesus Christ!

## The Ultimate Warrior

Jesus didn't kill anybody or do anything destructive. Yet He is the ultimate, authentic Warrior. He possessed everything from courage to fighting for a righteous cause, camaraderie, determination, victory, and glory.

In his book, *Healing the Masculine Soul,* Gordon Dalbey lists those qualities in his review of the warrior spirit. He recalls an article about the Green Berets in *Esquire* magazine, written by George Leonard: "They cited loyalty, patience, intensity, calmness, compassion and will. They agreed that the true warrior knows himself, knows his limitations . . . Self-mastery, according to the Special Forces men, is a warrior's central motivation. He is always practicing, always seeking to hone his skills, so as to become the best possible instrument for accomplishing his mission. The warrior takes calculated risks and tests himself repeatedly. He believes in something greater than himself: a religion, a cause. He may snivel (their word for complain), but he is not a victim."[2]

From those character qualities, Dalbey lists some questions you need to ask yourself (I've paraphrased them):

- When have I demonstrated loyalty to someone or some cause greater than myself?

- When have I shown patience during trial, disciplined intensity in a task, calmness under fire?

- What skills am I working to develop?

- When have I taken a calculated risk and tested myself?

- When have I taken the initiative to right a wrong?

- When have I demonstrated compassion by taking action on behalf of another person?[3]

Acting on the above questions will develop godly traits and inspire you to possess the spirit of a warrior. Whether you work at home, school, office, courtroom, or assembly line, you must possess this spirit. The battles will come. The question is: Will you be prepared?

### The Will to Prepare

As a Christian, the will to win is nothing without the will to prepare. The greatest tool to educate yourself for each level of life is the warrior's ultimate weapon: the Bible. You can compare its spiritual value to the physical test shown in 2 Samuel 23:9–10.

Eleazar is *the* role model for mighty men. When everyone else fled, he kept fighting until his hand froze to his sword. Then the Lord intervened and gave him the victory.

The limits of your destiny will be set by how much time you spend in the Word. You will not win battles without knowing what it means to stand in faith on the Word of God. Arm yourself with His Word and step toward maturity. Don't shrink back. Rewards from Christ represent riches worth more than any earthly possessions.

Are you ready to take the challenge? It is huge. Yet great honors await those who will stand up to proclaim the truth to today's younger generation, the one labeled Generation X.

### Gut Check

1. What weaknesses or negative circumstances does the devil constantly use to oppress you? List them. Next write out a strategic plan to overcome this opposition. For example, financial stability usually brought peace to my home, but problems brought on stress. I realized the stress came from lack of trust in God. I repented and now confidently expect the Lord to meet our needs. Another example is the mild emotional letdowns I used to suffer about 4 P.M. each day. I overcame that with simple adjustments in diet and exercise.

2. Do you seek a disciplined lifestyle? If not, follow these steps:

a. Start a Bible study notebook. Keep track of how long you spend in the Word each day.

b. Record what you learn from your readings.

c. Record specific prayer requests, such as people you are praying for or wisdom you need. Then record God's answers as they come.

3. What mountains exist in your life? Have you tried to climb them?

4. Are you in a lowly position? List some things you can learn from it.

5. Have you ever reached out to someone who struggles with the same kind of problems you do?

# 12

## GENERATION X

*Do you see a man skilled in his work? He will stand before kings; he will not stand before obscure men.*

*—Proverbs 22:29*

I REMEMBER WITNESSING TO A BASKETBALL player one time at Southern Cal. I pulled out all the stops, sharing my testimony, quoting verses that applied to his situation, and trying to persuade him the Lord offered a better way of life. Finally, he shrugged, "Tom, I can't accept Jesus Christ until I find myself." I replied: "Listen. You're never going to find yourself until you find Jesus Christ."

A generation searching for itself. That is how social commentators label today's under-thirty crowd: "Generation X." A name that signifies a group of people who don't know where they came from or where they are going, a generation groping for identity and purpose. The philosophy that captures this generation will revolutionize the world. For good or bad, whoever defines Generation X rules the future. Right now, theorists claim, it holds no distinguishing brand marks, has a cynical view of life, lacks ethics, harbors an unbridled passion for pleasure, and is the first generation that is relatively unchurched.

If you are part of this group (born from 1965 on), take heart. In the words of Esther 4:14, you have been placed here "for such a time as this." God has placed you in this time in history to provide answers for your lost, confused peers. He created you with a purpose. There are reasons for your existence at this time. You have something to do that will further God's kingdom. This is your destiny.

If you are a disciple of Jesus, you should be thrilled. You live in one of history's most challenging, opportune times. The 1990's critics of those under thirty call you a faceless, nameless, meaningless generation. Listen to these expressions of fatalistic trends from highly-respected educators:

- Samuel Hynes, professor of English at Princeton University says: "My students have been bright, but they seem to put on an education as though it were a Brooks Brothers suit that their fathers paid for. They don't see education as an opportunity to change the world."[1]

- Victor Herbert, director of New York City high schools says young people suffer from a growing malaise: "They feel they're not worth anything, they're not appreciated. And if you don't feel self-esteem, you tend to be a bit more reckless and a bit more careless."[2]

- A 1990 report by People for the American Way concluded that there is a "citizenship crisis" in which "America's youth are alarmingly ill-prepared to keep democracy alive in the 1990s and beyond."[3]

- The same report said: "It is a generation that knows less, cares less, votes less, and is less critical of its leaders and institutions than young people in the past . . . It is not so much that young adults under thirty are disillusioned, as they are uninterested."[4]

These are bleak-sounding statements. So what? That means you have the opportunity to influence the world positively, like no other generation of the past. Young man, I challenge you to enter the war for the hearts of this generation. The battle is under way. Ready or not, like it or not, or aware of it or not, you are part of it. It is the bitter struggle of two rivals for *your* future. The winner names the age! In this war for tomorrow's leaders, the outcome will shape the twenty-first century.

A couple years ago *Time* magazine said that Americans in their twenties sometimes seem to have an image but no impact: "The search is on for those who would give real meaning to this 'Virtual Generation,'" it wrote. "The 20-29 age bracket has so far been conceptualized more as a marketing tool than an active social force."[5]

In other words, others see Generation X as a group defined by fads instead of purpose. Even so, "baby busters" are fed up with the baby boomers' reckless and selfish stewardship of the future. The younger set stands by, ready and poised to take the wheel. But without God's guidance, they will simply crash and burn.

## Setting the Course

God reveals His purpose for this generation in Jeremiah 29:11–13, "'For I know the plans that I have for you,' declares the Lord, 'plans for welfare and not for calamity to give you a future and a hope. Then you will call upon Me and come and pray to Me, and I will listen to you. And you will seek Me and find Me, when you search for Me with all your heart.'"

Do you see from these words how much God cares for you? That is why a heart desperate to please the Lord is the number one ingredient in fulfilling your destiny. Matthew 5:13 (TLB) provides a much clearer definition of the responsibilities of Christ's disciples: "You are the world's seasoning, to make it tolerable. If you lose your flavor, what will happen to the world? And you yourselves will be thrown out and trampled underfoot as worthless."

As I mentioned in chapter 5, today many regard Christianity as worthless. Believers frequently face critics who laugh at the Bible as fairy tales or myths. A student at the University of Nevada at Reno told me, "My professor stood up on the first day of class and arrogantly said, 'You are a fool if you take the Bible literally.'" Not surprising that to hold godly traits today means that others will often treat you like you carry a disease and should be quarantined.

When the world flaunts its wickedness before the church and mocks God's people, without anyone raising a standard to oppose them, God is dishonored among men. When you tolerate society's sin and perversity, and do not take a stand, it is the same as joining in their sin. Silence condemns you as an accomplice.

I've said it before, but it's worth repeating: *What you tolerate you cannot change.* As the old saying goes, silence may be golden. But sometimes it's just plain yellow. The situation *is* black and white. You are either part of the solution or you are part of the problem. Jesus said so.

Reggie White took such a stand when he confronted a NBA superstar. Challenging his ungodly habits, both on and off the court, he encouraged the player to change for the sake of his duties as a role model. The man protested, "Nobody's paying me to be a role model." Reggie shot back this reply, "*You are a role model,* and one day you will be accountable to God for the good or the evil."

Our destiny is a gift from God. We must be good caretakers of it because the Lord will ultimately hold us responsible for our actions and the sphere of influence he has entrusted to us. When you repent of your wrongs and become a disciple of Jesus, it signals a new beginning. One of the benefits is the breaking of longtime family curses, such as alcohol abuse, lust, pride, divorce, and anger. This decision literally will be felt by the world!

## Destined to Win

One young man who shook his generation was Josiah, a king of Judah. He lived in an era very similar to the late twentieth century. The perverseness surrounding him in that society, more than six hundred years before Christ was born, included widespread homosexuality, immorality, idol worship, and active mediums and spiritists (wizards) much like our Psychic Hot Lines.

His testimony begins in 2 Kings 22:1–2: "Josiah was eight years old when he became king, and he reigned thirty-one years in Jerusalem . . . and *he did right in the sight of the Lord and walked in all of the way of his father David,* nor did he turn aside to the right or to the left" (italics added). Josiah had a clean slate. He lived a good, moral life in the midst of a wicked generation.

The story continues through verse 25 of the next chapter. His epitaph reads, "And before him there was no king like him who *turned to the Lord* with all his heart and with all his soul and with all his might, according to all the law of Moses; nor did any like him arise after him" (italics added).

Sound pretty ordinary? He was a nice guy, right? Well, you just missed the irony. If Josiah was so godly in chapter 22, why did chapter 23 say he turned to the Lord with all his might? When biblical figures turn towards God they have usually been pretty bad dudes. Since Josiah was so righteous, what could have happened? Why did the Bible credit him with turning to God like no other king?

The answer is that Josiah found the Book of the Law, which included the chronicles of Israel's history. The nation had treated it carelessly and lost it. (Pretty much the same way some today treat their Bible now, tossing it in the corner of their bedroom and ignoring it.) When the king dug it out, he saw these words in 1 Kings 13:2 which were written over 350 years before Josiah was born: "And he cried against the altar by the word of the Lord, and said, 'O altar, altar,' thus says the Lord, "Behold, a son shall be born to the house of David, Josiah by name; and on you he shall sacrifice the priests of the high places who burn incense on you, and human bones shall be burned on you."""

Well, imagine your feelings if you saw your own name spelled out in a prophecy given hundreds of years before. The discovery and reading of this book had a dramatic impact. Josiah learned that simply being a good, moral man wasn't enough. He saw that he had a call from God to impact his nation. He was part of the Lord's divine plan of redemption and world dominion. Though Josiah had been a good man, he tolerated gross sin (see 2 Kings 22:1–10). He had quit being "salt" in his world. He had hidden his light in the midst of darkness. He had to "come out of the closet" and speak up.

Likewise, it isn't good enough to just be a Christian in today's generation. You must press on to discover the purpose for which God created you. Then you must throw yourself into reaching this destiny with all your heart. Don't give me that old line, "My religion's a personal thing." Yeah, so personal no one even knows about it.

### No More Mr. Nice Guy

Josiah saw that he couldn't just be a pleasant guy any longer. Through God's Word, he saw the wickedness around him. He had no choice but to expose this darkness. Ephesians 5:11 outlines the same duty, "And do not participate in the unfruitful deeds of darkness, but instead even expose them."

Instead, most Christians try to be nicer than Jesus. Yes, He was kind and pleasant. But sin enraged Him. Because God has called us to impact the world, we must confront sin. As Psalm 94:16 asks, "Who will stand up for me against evildoers? Who will take his stand for me against those who do wickedness?"

Young man, you must carry the torch of righteousness and reformation to your generation. God has destined His people to change the spiritual climate in our country. As a disciple, your vision must stretch past personal salvation. God's heart is for the nations. He wants to see His rule influence the political arena, the arts, the media, education, medicine, sports, the economy, and all other areas of society.

Who is God going to employ for such an awesome task? The same people He always uses: Ordinary folks like you and me. When God's destiny comes over you, God's grace will give you the ability and determination to do it. Want a quick hint about your destiny? The problem that infuriates you the most is the one God has assigned you to solve.

"It was easy for Josiah to get excited," you may argue. "I would too if I saw my name and what I'm supposed to do in the Bible." Well, as a follower of Christ, don't you bear the name "Christian?" Your name is written all over the Bible, starting in the Lamb's book of life (as spelled out in Rev. 3:5). You are part of a chosen race, a royal priesthood. Consider these scriptures:

- Psalm 139:16: "Thine eyes have seen my unformed substance; and in Thy book they were all written, the days that were ordained for me, when as yet there was not one of them."

- Ephesians 1:5: "He predestined us to adoption as sons through Jesus Christ to Himself."

- Ephesians 2:10: "For we are His workmanship, created in Christ Jesus *for good works,* which God prepared beforehand, that *we should walk in them*" (italics added).

However, God will not reveal Himself and your destiny to the casual questioner. You must have the same heart and dedication that King Josiah demonstrated. His testimony lined up with Jesus' command in Matthew 22:37, "You shall love the Lord your God with all your heart, and with all your soul, and with all your mind."

Under the lordship of Jesus, you will be able to give God the best years of your life, while you are still young. Never forget to view your future with an eye on your destiny. The impact you make for God's kingdom will far outlast your natural, earthly life.

### Seeds of Greatness

Great events start with small, seemingly insignificant ones. The problem most people have is failing to see that great men who accomplish great things sprouted from small seeds. Take the story of Eric White.

Nicknamed "Night Crawler" because of his lifestyle of endless partying, his habits had led to a steadily declining athletic career as a pole vaulter. He avoided me the day I was preaching outdoors on the USC campus. While my message touched his heart, he thought: "Lord, I know need I get saved, but I'm not going to that man. He's a fanatic."

Turning away, he walked to the athletic building locker room, where he ran into Reggie Pendleton, a football defensive back and one of our ministry's best disciplers. He told Reggie he wanted to live for God and asked what he should do. Reggie said, "I got just the man you need to meet." Reggie grabbed him by the hand and brought Eric back to where I was preaching. White's mouth dropped open.

"This guy's a loser; he'll never make it," I thought when I first saw Eric that afternoon, sloppily dressed in ragged fatigues and no shirt, looking like he just rolled out of bed. But when he turned away from his rotten lifestyle, submitted himself to Jesus, and asked Christ to come into his heart, God took over. The Lord transformed Eric White into a two-time All-American, increasing his pole vaulting performances by two feet the first year. He went on to earn a master's degree from UCLA and married a graduate of Princeton University. Eric now serves in one of the nation's largest high school dropout prevention centers.

It all began with someone the world would write off as worthless. So I ask: What great possibilities await you? But remember, you too can change the world. Inside you rest the seeds of greatness. You will never make an impact without first creating a collision. Expect a battle. The devil hates a man who keeps his eye on his destiny.

Ed Cole often challenges audiences at his Christian men's meetings with this statement, "Men who lead determine to influence." God is looking for the rare breed of men who know they are in Christ and want to build His kingdom. Even the world secretly awaits such men. Don't get discouraged if it doesn't happen immediately. Keep reading God's Word, pray, and trust in the Lord to do the rest.

In addition, it helps to memorize some of the great promises from the Bible:

- Psalms 37:23, "The steps of a man are established by the Lord; and He delights in his way."

- First John 4:4, "Greater is He who is in you than he who is in the world."

- Joshua 1:8, "You shall meditate on [the Word] day and night, so that you may be careful to do according to all that is written in it; for then you will make your way prosperous, and then you will have success."

- Romans 8:16–17, "The Spirit Himself bears witness with our spirit that we are children of God, and if children, heirs also, heirs of God and fellow heirs with Christ, if indeed we suffer with Him in order that we may also be glorified with Him."

- Philippians 4:13, "I can do all things through Him who strengthens me."

- Matthew 19:26, "With God all things are possible.

- Mark 11:24, "All things for which you pray and ask, believe that you have received them, and they shall be granted you."

- Jeremiah 29:11, "'For I know the plans I have for you,'" declares the LORD, 'Plans for welfare and not for calamity to give you a future and a hope.'"

- Galatians 2:20, "I have been crucified with Christ; and it is no longer I who live, but Christ lives in me."

- Ephesians 2:6, "[God] raised us up with Him, and seated us with Him in the heavenly places, in Christ Jesus."

- Romans 8:37, "But in all things we overwhelmingly conquer through Him who loved us."

- First Peter 5:7, "[Cast] all your anxiety on Him, because He cares for you."

### Fulfill Your Destiny

If you choose to fulfill your destiny, then you can look forward to the future with joy. One day, when you depart from your earthly body and stand before the throne of your Heavenly Father, you can say: "Reporting back from duty, Father. Mission accomplished."

Without a purpose, you have no reason to live. Remember Benjamin Franklin's words (which I quoted in chap. 2), "Nine out of ten men are suicides." Don't throw away your life on trivial, meaningless pursuits without affecting the world for any future good. What a sad waste of God's gracious gift of life. Remember, destiny is not a matter of chance. It is a matter of choice. Choose wisely. And keep in mind that God sees you more favorably than you do yourself. Learn why in chapter 13.

### Gut Check

1. Are you a member of today's young generation? How do you feel about the label that's been attached to you?

2. Do you believe God has a purpose for your life? Do you believe He loves you? Why?

3. Does it take a "Superman" to solve problems?

4. Rewrite the destiny for your life. Has this Mission Statement changed or developed more fully since you began reading this book? How?

5. Do you have a full time call to reach this generation?

Would you like to tell me about it? Write to Tom Sirotnak, "Warriors," Morning Star Church, 1825 West Lomita Boulevard, Suite 440, Lomita, CA 90717.

# I CALLS 'EM AS I SEES 'EM

*One can never consent to creep when one feels an impulse to soar.*

*—Helen Keller[1]*

G UTZON BORGLUM, THE RENOWNED SCULPTOR of Mount Rushmore, was working on a bust of Abraham Lincoln. At first it wasn't clear to the woman hired to sweep out his studio. One day she recognized Lincoln's face emerging from nothingness. Surprised, she turned and asked Borglum, "How did you know that Mr. Lincoln was in that stone?"[2]

As the Master Artist, God doesn't look at us in our rough, limited, fallen state. He looks past the present with His divine, Fatherly eyes. He loves us for who we are and what we will become in Christ. Young men desperately need God's insight about themselves. After speaking in hundreds of American high schools and colleges and talking personally with students, I have discovered their number one fear is getting tagged with crude nicknames or labels.

Millions battle the early scars of rejection inflicted on them by cruel classmates or insensitive authority figures.

As I mentioned earlier, I struggled with peer acceptance after being labeled as a young boy. "Slow learner," "uncoordinated," and "chunky" were a few of my nicer nicknames. Given statistics and my experience, I wasn't surprised when I asked a packed auditorium of 3,000 students at a Southern California high school if they liked themselves—and 95 percent responded, "No." Yet this does not square with the truth. As a young man, you must never forget that:

- God has created you and He loves you.

- You have a purpose and destiny in life.

- Because you are His creation and He has created you for a purpose, you have great value.

God doesn't value you based on your popularity, your clothes, your looks, how many trophies you own, or your great feats of strength. All this amounts to is "high gloss." Edwin Louis Cole once commented, "It's true of knives, furniture, and women. . . the higher the gloss, the cheaper the merchandise." And so it holds ture about men. You don't need to put on a false image with God. Be real. He values you for you, just the way you are. If you have been born again you are part of a royal family. It doesn't matter what people say about you. What matters is what God says.

When the Lord rejected Saul as king over Israel because of his disobedience, He told Samuel to select a king from the family of Jesse (1 Sam. 16:1–7). When Samuel saw Jesse's first son, handsome and rugged Eliab, he thought that surely this must be God's anointed. But the Lord corrected him, saying, "Do not look at his appearance or at the height of his stature, because I have rejected him; for God sees not as man sees, for man looks at the outward appearance, but the Lord looks at the heart" (v. 7). God was looking for a man after His own heart, the "apple of His eye." So He picked David, the least of his family, which in turn was the lowest of Israel's families.

It would have been easy for the least of the least to give up because of others' low opinion of him. But David was faithful. Because of that, God lifted him to greatness. Fame can spring up in an instant, a single act, but greatness takes a lifetime. God has called you to be a great young man. It requires a lifetime of total commitment. Can you be that kind of man? If so, God may give you a new name that will fit your new purpose.

## What's in a Name?

To answer the above question: A lot! Historically, a person's name signified occupation or family lineage. Throughout the Bible the Lord renames people. Why? To change their self-concept and self-image. Their new name reflected their life's mission.

So, Abram, meaning "exalted father," became Abraham, or "father of a multitude of nations" (Gen. 17:5). And this was before he and Sarah even had any children. Not to mention that both of them were well past childbearing years; Abraham was pushing 100, and Sarah, 90. Remember, your background, shortcomings, or circumstances don't limit God's power. He calls 'em as He sees 'em. What name will God bestow upon you?

Proverbs 23:7 contains a principle that is true in a man's heart: "For as he thinks within himself, so he is." You have heard the old saying, "You are what you eat." But the Word declares, "You are what you think." I see too many Christians on college campuses and elsewhere walking around defeated and weighed down by guilt and condemnation. They have developed a "sin conscience" instead of a "righteous conscience."

A "sin conscience" dwells on every little thing you have ever done wrong. Under this burden, you become so introspective you cannot get past repentance. You are so afraid of not pleasing the Lord that you can't experience the abundant life promised by Jesus. You miss the benefits of the cleansing power of the cross.

Instead of focusing on the negative, we must see ourselves in light of God's Word. If our hearts are right and under His lordship, God sees us the way we are going to be one day in heaven—holy and perfect. That is more real to Him than our present imperfections.

Romans 12:2 says you can be transformed "by the renewing of your mind." In other words, I am what the Word says I am, I have what the Word says I have, and I will become what the Word says I will become. You must reconstruct the way you think about yourself. Use God's Word instead of the world's measures.

Godly character traits in the Bible are for you. If you struggle with fear, rejection, or insignificance, go to God's Word. Take the promises of the Scriptures as personal! Second Peter 1:4 says, "He has granted to us His precious and magnificent promises, in order that by them you might become partakers of the divine nature, *having escaped the corruption that is in the world by lust*" (italics added). Do you see the significance of that? The Word will gradually transform you into the mirror image of God's character. Then you will stop being a slave to worldly habits.

## The Image

Like I said before, Andre Agassi's boast, "Image is everything," is true, in a biblical sense. The images a man carries in his heart will become reality. The principle from the Bible is that everything produces after its own kind. In other words, you become what you think about and who you hang around.

Sadly, young men have seen too many lousy portrayals of manhood. Movies, television, books, and other media belch out a stream of anti-God, anti-masculine messages. Destruction of positive, godly images in our national mentality has inflicted emotional sickness on society.

The TV and film industries have powerful influence in shaping the ideal of a "real man" today. The vulgar, sex-crazed, macho, and independent stud (yet, ironically, sensitive) is Hollywood's stereotype of a man headed into the twenty-first century. When people criticize the producers of warped images, they argue, "We don't have power over the minds of people." But these hypocrites will boldly guarantee product sales for advertisers willing to cough up a few hundred thousand dollars for a thirty-second commercial. Images give birth to substance.

As men, we have suffered from overexposure to the world's images of genuine manhood. We also suffer from too much emphasis on "group think," or social justification. This occurs when a group or clique determines right and wrong. I've seen this happen constantly on athletic teams and in social clubs or fraternities. "If you want to be in the norm, part of the in-crowd, you'll be like us," they brag. What you become is a social clone, one who looks like, acts like, and talks like everyone else. And it's the wrong pattern to follow.

When I was at USC, social status meant everything. Too many non-frat guys held second-class citizenship, unless, of course, you were an athlete. In this clone system, a "real man" drank gallons of beer, chased women, and acted like an animal. He lived up to the image of the upper-class, in-tune, politically conservative yet socially liberal. The truth is, once you got past the rituals, 90 percent of these men were shallow, self-consumed, insecure, empty, and hopeless.

Group-think people laugh at truth and mock those who proclaim it. They can't stand alone in their worship of vain images, so they band together and become "clone cronies." It takes a real man to break away from this herd mentality. The kind described in 1 Peter 4:3–5, "For the time already past is sufficient for you to have carried out the desire of the Gentiles, having pursued a course of sensuality, lusts, drunkenness, carousals, drinking parties and abominable idolatries. And in all this, *they are surprised* that you do not run with them into the same excess of dissipation [note: indulging in pleasure to the point of harming yourself], and they malign you; but they shall give account to Him who is ready to judge the living and the dead" (italics added). And you thought the Bible didn't have anything relevant to say about today!

Don't let Satan destroy your masculinity. Be a man after God's own heart. After all, He created you in His image. Image emerges from whom you identify with. This is important for three reasons:

- Every man is in a desperate search for an identity. His identity makes him unique and adds definition to his existence.

- A man also craves identity so he will have something on which to pattern his life. He is not truly secure unless he identifies with, or follows, a higher ideal or standard than himself. We see this in children, who naturally mimic their father or passionately imitate their favorite sports star.

- A man seeks identity to gain acceptance. He will not feel adequate until he can fit into a societal mold. Men are attracted to groups.

Decide today that, as a man of God, you will not identify with anyone or anything other than Jesus Christ and our Heavenly Father. He is the One who will give you definition, security, and acceptance.

## Designer Labels

Unfortunately, millions seek designer lifestyles that will supposedly link them with high society. So young boys are willing to kill for name-brand athletic shoes so they can "be like Mike" (Michael Jordan). But shoes don't make the man. Heart does. Mike may be a great guy, but he can't do anything for you. For that matter, neither can I. Jesus can, if you will imitate Him and become His ambassador. Life is a grindstone. Whether it grinds you down or polishes you depends on whom you are following.

Luke 4:18 describes one primary aim of Jesus' ministry as to bring "recovery of sight to the blind." Not just physical sight, but how you see yourself in a proper, biblical perspective. It is crucial that you see yourself as Christ sees Himself in us. Many will never walk in victory because they can't see themselves that way. Failure, insult, fear, and shortcomings blind them. The result is doom. Proverbs 29:18a (AMP) says, "Where there is no vision [no redemptive revelations of God], the people perish."

Do you realize that Jesus holds a vision for you right now? King, priest, overcomer, ruling and reigning in His strength and crowned in righteousness . . . those are just a few of the scriptural descriptions of you! Impossible? How could Jesus call Peter—who later crumbled under pressure— "the rock?" Or James and John the "sons of thunder?" The Lord branded Thomas, whose general reputation is that of a doubter, "the great apostle of faith." Moses, stripped of pride and self-worth, asked, "Who am I, that I should go to Pharaoh, and that I should bring the sons of Israel out of Egypt?" (Ex. 3:11). And God sent him anyway.

Young man, God is calling you. Just like Moses, He is saying: "I've called you out of darkness and into My light. You are the head and not the tail. You are a conqueror through My son, Jesus. It doesn't matter what labels or tags the world sticks on you. Rise up! Be My man for this generation!"

## The Chicken Eagle

I remember a story my associate pastor shared early in my Christian walk. It was about a man who went through the forest, seeking great birds. He caught a young eagle, brought it home and placed the bird among his chickens, ducks, and turkeys. He even gave it chicken feed to eat.

Five years later a naturalist came to visit the man. After walking through his garden, he said, "That bird over there is an eagle."

"Yes," said the owner, "but I have trained it to be a chicken. Though his wing span measures fifteen feet, he's no longer an eagle."

The naturalist shook his head, "No. It's an eagle. He has the heart of an eagle. I will make it soar to the heavens."

"No way," the owner said, "it is a chicken and it will never fly."

Finally, they agreed to a test. The naturalist picked up the eagle and told him, "You belong to the sky. Stretch forth your wings and fly."

The eagle looked up, but when he glanced back down and saw the chickens feeding, he jumped down to eat. The owner said, "I told you he was a chicken."

"No, it is an eagle," said the naturalist. "Give it another chance tomorrow."

The next day the naturalist took the great bird to the top of the house. "Eagle, stretch forth your wings and fly." Again, the eagle saw the chickens feeding and jumped down.

"I told you it was a chicken," grinned the owner.

"No way," the naturalist repeated. "Give him one more chance. Tomorrow he will fly."

The next morning the naturalist rose at dawn and drove the eagle to the foot of a high mountain. The rising sun bathed the mountaintop in gold. Every crag of the rocks glistened in the breathtaking morning. Picking up the bird, the naturalist said, "You are an eagle. You belong in the sky, soaring high, not on the earth. Stretch forth your wings and fly."

The eagle glanced around and trembled, as if new life were entering its body. Still it did not fly. Then the naturalist made it look straight at the sun. Suddenly the eagle stretched out its wings and with a screech mounted high into the air. As it circled it rose higher and higher, never to return. Though confined from its natural habitat and tamed so it would act a chicken, at heart it was still an eagle.[3]

Young man, God created you in His image, with the grace and strength of an eagle. But Satan's chief goal is to make you think you are a chicken. Don't settle for chicken feed. Thank God that you can focus on the Son, who is brighter than the natural sun. Jesus will cause you to rise to new heights. It is time to spread your wings and fly. As Isaiah 40:31a says, "Yet those who wait for the Lord . . . will mount up with wings like eagles."

God wants you to see yourself not in weakness, but power. Man is like a tack: He can only go as far as his head will let him. If you have been born again, Almighty God resides in you. Your past failures or weaknesses don't matter. After all, it is much better to look where you're going than see where you've been. Dare to march on and become all you can with God! "Arise, shine; for your light has come, and the glory of the LORD has risen upon you" (Isa. 60:1).

## Skyscraper Theology

"Christ in you, the hope of glory" (Col. 1:27b).

With the world's influence so widespread via modern communications, staying God-minded is a challenge. Yet it is one you must tackle. Colossians 2:10 says that "in Him you have been made complete." That means now!

Christian man, you have the spiritual genetic makeup of a champion for Christ, who is holy and perfect. Think of it as an apple seed. Despite its tiny appearance, on the inside this seed contains the genetic imprint that will enable it to grow into a powerful, fruitful, fifteen-foot-tall, apple tree. Everything this future giant needs is in that seed. The only ingredients lacking are time and nourishment.

You say you're no apple tree and don't have any seeds inside you? That isn't what the Bible says. Consider these verses.

- First Peter 1:23: "You have been born again not of seed which is perishable but imperishable, that is, through the living and abiding word of God." The power of the seed will do the work if you give it time and nourishment.

151

- Philippians 2:13: "For it is God who is at work in you, both to will and to work for His good pleasure."

- Philippians 1:6b: "He who began a good work in you will perfect it until the day of Christ Jesus."

It is because of this perfect seed within you that you can boldly proclaim the words of Philippians 4:13, "I can do all things through Him who strengthens me."

God has given you eternal life and victory over death, calls you more than a conqueror in Christ, and says in Him you are complete. So quit valuing your low self-opinion over God's. "I can't," "I never could," "I never will," "I'm just not able," and "I'll never make it" are rehearsals for failure. You're securing your future with doubt and unbelief. These negative self-images are like running a video through your mind, over and over and over. You must learn, as 2 Corinthians 5:7 says, to "walk by faith, not by sight."

A perfect example of greatness arising from nothing is a skyscraper. It starts as a mere thought in an architect's mind. That architect has to have faith, the initial creative force that gives substance to his design. Faith leads to initiative, which leads to industry, which leads to the completion of a vision. And so it can be with you. Hebrews 11:10 says of Abraham, "For he was looking for the city which has foundations, whose architect and builder is God." God wants to be your Chief Architect, the Designer of your character and the Engineer of your dreams. With the foundation of His Word, which contains His promises, you will reach completion in every aspect of life.

This is my prayer for you:

Dear Lord, give us mighty men who are strong, decisive and consistent. Men of vision and destiny who dare to see themselves as you see them. Conquering warriors who are secure in their identity and confident of their masculinity. Let them not cower in insecurity, be intimidated by failure, or fall to feelings of insignificance. Let them be daring men of courage who will declare they are strong in the Lord, and glory in the cross. As they come into their land of promises, I pray they would not shrink back like the spies of Israel, who fainted at the sight of tall men. Bless all of those who read this with a great inheritance. I pray that they would know the truth of Psalms 118:6, "The Lord is for me; I will not fear." In Jesus' name, amen.

## Live Up to the Name

Christian men, by the working of the Holy Spirit, release your faith, speak His Word, and then watch out. You will never be the same! I believe that God wants to give many of you a new name. Strong labels, like "man of faith," or "valiant warrior." Maybe "prophet to the nation," or, like Nathanael in John 1:47, man of "no guile."

Often the literal translation of your first or last name will give you a clue. Thomas, my first name, means "double" or "twin." James, my middle name, means "supplanter." It is defined as, "To violently uproot by force and replace with something better." When I learned this, I saw that I was a "double supplanter."

Then the Lord led me to Jeremiah 1:5–12, where the prophet Jeremiah describes how God promised to speak through him, deliver him from trouble, and appoint him to be over kingdoms and nations. That became my definitive Scripture. It was for me! Supplanting the works of the devil with works that glorify my Father. That became the strong foundation for discovering the purpose for my life.

What about you? Go look it up. Christian bookstores carry books that define the meanings of names from A to Z. But don't stop there. Seek the full revelation of your identity in the Bible. Maybe you find yourself continually drawn to a certain personality or character trait. That is a good indication of the type of spirit God desires to manifest in you.

Dare to believe that, as a man thinks of himself, so he will be, and that you can become a strong man. Fill your mind with God's Word, take charge over your thoughts, and let the new you surface. Then you will be ready to become a champion. Read on to the last chapter about these masculine heroes.

### Gut Check

1. What crude nicknames or putdowns have you endured from others? How does that make you feel? Look up Psalm 18:21. Repeat it aloud and declare who you are in Christ.

2. Describe your self-image. How did you develop it?

3. Do you always go along with the crowd or are you a leader?

4. How do you view your masculinity?

5. Are the seeds of greatness inside of you? Why?

6. What does your name mean? How does that affect the way you look at yourself?

# 14

## CHAMPIONS

*Champions are not those who never fail. They are those who never quit.*

—*Edwin Louis Cole*

THOSE WHO STAY WILL BE CHAMPIONS. The sign hung in bold letters over the locker room door. I needed the reminder before another gut-busting USC football practice. Facing future NFL stars like Marcus Allen, Don Mosebar, Bruce Matthews, and Keith Van Horn took courage. Quitting crossed my mind more than once.

That was nothing, though, compared to the courage I needed to raise my hand in front of my friends and identify with Christ. Ephesians 4:21–24 says, "If indeed you have heard Him . . . in reference to your former manner of life, you lay aside the old self . . . *and put on the new self*, which in the likeness of God has been created in righteousness and holiness of the truth" (italics added). That night I heard this message from the Lord: "You were dedicated to playing football, but you'll have to be twice as committed to serving Me!"

Serving Jesus Christ in this Christian-bashing era takes guts. I wish every church hung the same banner over its doors: *THOSE WHO STAY WILL BE CHAMPIONS.* Jesus put it this way in Revelation 2:7 and 26, "To him who overcomes, I will grant to eat of the tree of life, which is in the Paradise of God" and " . . . to Him I will give authority over the nations."

God has given you the tools to overcome. In every man's heart He has placed the desire—called your ego—to be a warrior, champion, hero, and conqueror. Feminists want to kill this element of God-given masculinity. They label most men sexists or chauvinists. Now, some of this criticism is justified. Worldly men regularly use their ego to satisfy their lusts, pump up their pride, and exploit women.

But the Father doesn't want you to kill your ego. He wants you to sanctify it and bring it under the Holy Spirit's control. The spiritually-controlled ego is a driving force that causes men to dream and do great exploits—not for their selfish glory, but to honor their Master.

### Courage

It takes courage to be a radical activist for God. Courage is a by-product of convictions, meaning what you believe. Courage is defined as, "Bravery, that quality of mind which enables men to encounter danger and difficulties with firmness and without fear of depression of spirit." Let's face it, it takes courage to:

- Face reality

- Admit you have needs

- Make needed changes

- Reach tough decisions

- Hold to your convictions

- Accept responsibility

This is what it takes to be a man of God. It lines up with Paul's instruction to Timothy to show himself a man and not let anyone look down on his youthfulness. You may remember this from chapter two—to live above reproach you must establish good character, reputation, ethics, morality, and habits.

Moral courage is defined as, "The quality that enables a person to encounter hatred, disapproval, and contempt without departing from what is right." A real man always stands up for the truth. Moral cowardice means you will shrink from duty, danger, and pain, or yield to fear.

Godly courage responds to fear head on, never thinking of retreat. Consider an officer under the great military leader, Napoleon. This legendary general called Marshall Ney one of the bravest men he had ever known. But even the brace have their moments. One day Ney's knees trembled so badly before the battle he struggled to mount his horse. When he was finally in the saddle he shouted contemptuously, "Shake away, knees, you would shake worse than that if you knew where I am going to take you."

Courage doesn't mean you won't experience fear. It means fear won't control you. Fear is a natural emotion. What you do with fear determines whether you are brave or cowardly. I've heard it said, "A hero is no braver than anyone else; he's only braver five minutes longer."

### Get into the Game

In Joshua 1:2, God said to young Joshua, "Moses My servant is dead; now therefore arise." In other words: "Joshua, it's your turn. You've been a spectator long enough. Get in there now and lead My people." That is what God is saying to you: "Get in there and do it!"

You don't have to be perfect. Ever hear the humorous story about the baseball team that needs a man who plays every position perfectly, never strikes out, and never makes an error? The only problem is that there is no way to make him put down his hot dog and come out of the stands.

Too often this is exactly what happens in church. Spectators and second-guessers sit back and criticize those who do. Instead of just hearing what God has done for others, why not step into the arena of life so you have a testimony? Not a story of the great things you did, but about God's power at work in your life.

It is time to experience God and see Him move on your behalf. The baton is passing from one generation to the next. Some great men of faith, are in the twilight of life; others have already died. That means the younger generation must step up to fill the void. You say you are only 18, or 22, or 25? Young man, when do you think great men established their foundation for the future?

## Go Beyond Self

God called on Joshua to become the next link in the chain of Christianity. He knew how intimidating it would be to follow Moses, one of history's greatest men. So three times in Joshua, chapter 1, God tells him, "Be strong and courageous." Joshua needed courage to complete his mission. He got it by trusting God and relying on His power. The Lord stressed that success or failure revolved around the key factor of His Word. Joshua had to study it, rely on it, stand on it, and believe in it.

Do you see what mattered? Not this man's talent, but God's ability and power in him. As a young warrior, what makes the difference is not your extraordinary strength, but that same incredible force. Past failures, mistakes, or self-image don't matter. The only question is: Are you willing to obey God?

Every day you skip reading the Bible, it's like you telling God, "No, thanks, I'll get my own instruction." It takes courage and discipline to meet the Lord in His Word daily. Joshua had to crave it. God told him (Josh. 1:8), "This book of the law shall not depart from your mouth, but you shall meditate on it day and night, so that you may be careful to do according to all that is written in it; for then you will make your way prosperous, and then you will have success." (Read the rest of the chapter on your own.)

Holding to God's Word will bring success and help you stand against the waves of peer pressure and man-pleasers. President Theodore Roosevelt once said, "It is not the critic who counts, not the person who points out where the doer of deeds could have done better. The credit belongs to the person who is actually in the arena; whose face is marred by dust and sweat and blood; who strives valiantly; who errs and comes up short again and again; who knows the great enthusiasms, the devotions, and spends himself in a worthy cause; who at best knows in the end the triumph of high achievement; and at the worst, at least fails while daring greatly; so that his or her place shall never be with those cold and timid souls who know neither victory or defeat."[1]

## Stand Up

Years ago, Nikita Khrushchev, at the time premier of the Soviet Union, addressed the Supreme Soviet (similar to our Congress). He criticized the late Josef Stalin, the brutal Soviet dictator who slaughtered millions. As Khrushchev spoke, someone sent a note to the podium, asking, "What were you doing when Stalin committed these atrocities?" Khrushchev shouted, "Who sent up that note?" No one stirred. He added, "I'll give him one minute to stand up!" Nobody batted an eyelash. "All right," he said, "I'll tell you what I was doing. Exactly what the writer of this note is doing—nothing! I was afraid to be counted."[2]

Peer pressure can be overwhelming. At school, work place, or social events it can cause us to deny Jesus and do things we never dreamed of doing. Before I enrolled at USC, I vowed not to drink, smoke dope, or have sex before I got married. By the end of my first year, each of those values had vanished. An insatiable need for my fraternity brothers' approval led me to pull stunts that could have gotten me arrested, thrown in jail, and expelled—just to impress the guys. How stupid! But without God, I didn't know any other way to fit in and build my self-esteem.

Giving in to peer pressure causes you to become a moral coward and shut up instead of speak up. Take the story that John Jacobs, leader of the Power Team, tells about two upper-middle-class teenage girls in the Midwest. They plotted to stab their teacher because she had embarrassed them. The whole class looked on as they waited beside the door. No one said a word. Fortunately, the principal discovered the plot through a girl standing outside the room, shaking, and crying.

If you're faced with this kind of situation, will you sit back and watch someone die? Or speak up? What will you do if someone tells you to harm another person? Commit murder? In 1993, a seventeen-year-old man in Dallas, Texas, was sentenced to life in prison for firebombing an apartment and killing a fifteen-year-old. The defendant's attorney argued his client was just a scared kid, intimidated into committing the act by another gang member.

That seventeen-year-old may have been frightened. But how worse off is he now? Peer pressure is *no* defense for doing wrong; *never* an excuse for failing to do what is right. If fear causes you to shrink from doing right, despite the personal cost, you are a coward. As Proverbs 25:26 says, "Like a trampled spring and a polluted well is a righteous man who gives way before the wicked."

### Die to Self

Jesus warned against timidity in Matthew 10:32–33: "Everyone therefore who shall confess Me before men, I will also confess him before My Father who is in heaven. But whoever shall deny Me before men, I will also deny him before My Father who is in heaven." Denying God involves sins of commission (things you do) and omission, or things you fail to do.

That may mean withstanding peer pressure, including your family's. If you don't pick up that cross (the burden of opposition from loved ones) and follow Jesus, you cannot be His disciple. A man who picks up a cross symbolizes a death blow to self. The interesting thing about a dead man is that you can't scare him. When you die to self, you can be bold for Jesus.

Boldness is courage in action. Take Joaquin Barnett. We met when he was a linebacker at the University of Hawaii. Inspired by the gospel message, he and several other men decided to make four-foot-tall wooden crosses to identify with Christ and show other students the meaning of Easter. That didn't satisfy Joaquin, though. He wanted a "man size" cross.

That week Joaquin set out for his first class. He was ten minutes late. After all, carrying an eight-foot cross takes time. Since the students had begun the day's quiz, the thud, thud, thud of the cross echoed across the silent auditorium. When he reached his seat, his professor stared at him.

"Mr. Barnett, would you mind telling us what this cross is all about?" he demanded. For the next fifteen minutes, Joaquin boldly shared the message that salvation comes only through the name of

Jesus. He wasn't afraid to face the crowd and identify himself with Christ. And no one called him a wimp.

## Be Discipled

The quality I value most is humility. That means I am open to the leaders God ordained over me. It takes courage to be discipled. You must let down your guard and allow others who love you to inspect your life. You must be teachable and open to correction. You can't be defensive, in denial, or try to justify yourself.

Courage must be directed through discipleship. You must know what is right, proper, and biblically sound to know what to yield to and what to resist. Discipleship will put backbone in you, enabling you to proclaim Christ, stand on His Word, and live a holy life. Soft men cannot take tough times. They compromise. The world cries out for men who will be ruthlessly courageous and defeat compromise, lukewarmness, and sin!

A few years ago, I received the medal of valor from the Christian Men's Network. Founder Ed Cole presented me this honor for showing strong character and having courage to make a bold stand for God among the youth of this generation.

The next day, Greg Ball, founder and president of Champions for Christ, commented to some athletes: "You saw Tom get that medal last night, but you didn't see how he got it. I remember him as a young man at USC. He was voted 'Most Likely to Be Rebuked.' Tom was in the pastor's office so much, it was like having a revolving door on the office. He blew it a lot. But he was teachable. He was willing to change. He didn't give up. That's why he was honored last night."

It hurt to admit he was telling the truth. Yet that helped me remain transparent. When you are transparent everyone can see the real you. With nothing left to hide, you can grow. Long ago I vowed to continue to learn no matter how "big" an evangelist I became. I will always seek correction and discipleship.

In his prime, Muhammad Ali was about to take off on an airplane. When the stewardess reminded him to fasten his seat belt, he replied brashly, "Superman don't need no seat belt." She quickly shot back, "Superman don't need no airplane either." [3]

When it comes to discipleship, none of us are "Superman." Discipleship is the seat belt for Christ-likeness. Find a church where you can build strong friendships with other men and sit under a ministry that loves you enough to get involved with your life. From marriage to fatherhood to character to ethics, be transparent.

## Get Up

Even winners get tripped up occasionally. It is not a sin to fail. It is a sin to wallow in it. The Bible says, "For a righteous man falls seven times, and rises again" (Prov. 24:16). Remember all the times you failed? You stumbled all over the floor when you first tried to walk. You nearly drowned the first time you tried to swim. You missed the ball by a mile the first time you swung a bat.

You aren't alone, either. Everyone knows about Macy's Thanksgiving Day Parade. Are you aware that R.H. Macy failed seven times before his store caught on? Henry Ford went bankrupt twice. English novelist John Creasy got 753 rejection slips before publishing 564 books. Home run hero Babe Ruth, with 714 round trippers, also struck out 1,330 times. Don't worry about failure. Worry about the chances you miss when you won't even try.

Failure is not stumbling and falling. It's staying on the floor. Success comes from finding something while you are lying down that will help you stand up. Look at William Levine. After robbers held up his Brooklyn butcher shop four times in a month, he bought a bullet proof vest. Other business owners asked where they could get one, so he started taking orders as a sideline. That was how Body Armor International began, eventually expanding to a network of forty sales representatives and sales of more than five hundred vests per month.

Does that sound too amazing for you to accomplish? Take courage from Micah 7:7, where he said, "But as for me, I will watch expectantly for the Lord; I will wait for the God of my salvation. My God will hear me." Isn't that great news? When everyone else deserts you, leaving you feeling like a failure, God waits. And listens. Micah continues in verse 8: "Do not rejoice over me, O my enemy. Though I fall I will rise; Though I dwell in darkness, the Lord is a light for me." Even in Micah's darkest hour he refused to quit.

You should never fall without immediately thinking, *Get up.* I learned that in high school through trying to impress one of our cheerleaders. My crush on her motivated me to keep coming out for football, since fourth string wasn't that exciting. Desperately wanting her to notice me, I thought of a way to get her attention. The big homecoming game was coming up. Since I had little chance of seeing action, I thought, *I'll be the first to runthrough the 'Go Bruins' banner they hold up at the start of the game.*

A deceptively slow runner, I made sure to grab a spot in front of the pack. Then I took off early to get a ten-yard head start. The crowd cheered wildly as I headed for the banner. By the time I reached it, the rest of the team was nipping at my heels. Quickly glancing at the girl of my dreams, I gave a smile and a wink as I was the first one to explod through the paper barrier. Wham! One problem, though. When I looked at her, my feet got tangled up. I created my first impression face down in the mud. Head over heels I rolled, creating a domino effect. Two-thirds of my teammates joined me on the ground.

Remember your most embarrassing moment in life? That was mine. But the instant I realized I was going to fall, I thought, *You idiot! Get up!* Jumping to my feet, I hoped no one would notice I caused the pile-up. Fat chance. Not only do you have to get up when life knocks you down, I learned that embarrassment may hurt, but it won't kill you. Whenever we stumble we have to get up. Thomas Edison never would have invented the light bulb if he had allowed dozens of setbacks to stop him. So let your light shine!

## Rebounding

Getting knocked down is a normal part of life. How you rebound determines whether you are a winner or a loser. Sometimes the greatest men in history rise from the ashes of humiliation and defeat. Don't get hung up on past failures. See with the eye of faith and put your trust in Almighty God. He is a master at turning the humble into heroes.

Abraham Lincoln's leadership brought this nation through the Civil War intact. But he wasn't always known as a great man.

Lincoln's road to success featured many setbacks and heartbreak. Look at his resume:

1831: Failed in business.
1832: Defeated for state legislature.
1833: Second time failed in business.
1836: Suffered nervous breakdown.
1838: Defeated for Speaker.
1840: Defeated for Elector.
1843: Defeated for Congress.
1848: Defeated for Congress.
1855: Defeated for Senate.
1856: Defeated for Vice-president.
1858: Defeated for Senate.
1860: Elected President of the United States.

Champions don't give up. They get up. That is a vital element of Christian character. Where would we be today if Abraham Lincoln had not gotten up? How would history have changed? Would slavery still be legal?

When God says fight the good fight of faith, I believe He means, "Hey, you may have lost a battle, but you will still win the war." Make a decision right now that if you fall, whether by temptation, mistake, or injury, you will arise! Remember: if you find a path with no obstacles, it usually doesn't lead anywhere.

I will leave you with this poem by Robert Service that depicts the heart of a champion for Christ. This one is best read aloud—with boldness. As its title says, "Carry on!"

## CARRY ON

It's easy to fight when everything's right,
And you're mad with the thrill and the glory;
It's easy to cheer when victory's near,
And wallow in fields that are gory.
It's a different song when everything's wrong,
When you're feeling infernally mortal,
When it's ten against one, and hope there is none,
Buck up, little soldier, and chortle:
Carry on! Carry on!

There isn't much punch in your blow.
You're glaring and staring and hitting out blind;
You're muddy and bloody, but never you mind.
Carry on! Carry on!
You haven't the ghost of a show.
It's looking like death, but while you've a breath,
Carry on, my son! Carry on!

And so in the strife of the battle of life
It's easy to fight when you're winning;
It's easy to slave, and starve and be brave,
When the dawn of success is beginning.
But the man who can meet despair and defeat
With a cheer, there's the man of God's choosing;
The man who can fight to Heaven's own height
Is the man who can fight when he's losing.

Carry on! Carry on!
Things never were looming so black.
But show that you haven't a cowardly streak,
And though you're unlucky you never are weak.
Carry on! Carry on!
Brace up for another attack.
It's looking like hell, but — you never can tell;
Carry on, old man! Carry on!

There are some who drift out in the deserts of doubt,
And some who in brutishness wallow;
There are others, I know, who in piety go
Because of a Heaven to follow.
But to labor with zest, and to give of your best,
For the sweetness and joy of the giving;
To help folks along with a hand and a song;
Why, there's the real sunshine of living.
Carry on! Carry on!

Fight the good fight and true;
Believe in your mission, greet life with a cheer;
There's big work to do, and that's why you are here.
Carry on! Carry on!

Let the world be the better for you;
And at last when you die, let this be your cry:
*Carry on, my soul! Carry on!*

—*Robert Service*[4]

### Gut Check

1. When you face a tough task, do you stick with it or walk away?

2. How can you use your ego to serve God?

3. What is your definition of courage? How can you be brave?

4. What foundation are you laying for the future?

5. Describe a failure in your life. What have you done to overcome it?

6. What has God spoken to you about doing to further His kingdom? For example, getting involved in personal witnessing, the pro-life movement, or a sexual abstinence campaign. List the steps you will take to carry out His instructions.

# EPILOGUE

G OD HAS CALLED US AS HIS PEOPLE to reflect the victory that His Son won on the cross. God wants His people, His men, to live a lifestyle of victory. He wants us to be conquerors, not merely survivors. In God's Word, He promises us the grace we need to live free—from oppression, fear, and the sins that will pull us down into despair and defeat. The Lord is looking for warriors who want to live by faith, seize His promises, and walk in the best He has.

*Warriors* is a challenge to young men everywhere to grow up into everything God has for their lives and become firmly planted in the faith. Is that what you want? If so, are you willing to follow Christ and fight for His ways? The only way we can live in victory is when we seek God and come to know Him on His terms.

Jesus had a lot of people running after Him when He healed the sick, fed the hungry, and mesmerized the crowds with His wisdom. But every time He warned of the high price of discipleship, the masses walked away. His message was simple: We must take up our cross and deny self to follow Him. He didn't soothe us with words like, "I'm coming to walk with you" or "I'm coming in to your life to make it easier." He made it clear by saying (I'm paraphrasing): "If you love your life for My sake, you'll find it. But if you try to find it yourself, you can't help but mess up and lose it."

Following after Jesus with your whole heart by dying to selfish desires and living to do God's will serves as the foundation for your Christian walk. Christian soldier, there will always be tests of your foundation. You will experience days of feeling bad. Days when you struggle with guilt and condemnation. Times when you feel like a complete failure and unworthy of God's blessings and love.

Unfortunately, with defeated Christians, this becomes a way of life. Their identity becomes synonymous with misery as they are tossed from crisis to crisis, and prove unable to overcome the conflicts in their lives. Nothing will ever change until you choose to stand up and, based on the Bible's authority, declare otherwise.

Do you know what excites me today? The reality that:

- no matter how bad my situation looks

- no matter how inferior I may feel

- no matter how badly I have failed

- no matter how many mistakes I have made or will make

My faith is in God, and His constant, faithful love will always carry me into experiencing His abundant life. This allows me to praise God every day. Not because everything is "peachy keen" and I don't have any problems. Sometimes problems seem like a way of life. But I can praise God because I know, in the long run, if I don't quit and abandon ship, I can't lose.

Look around at the millions of broken homes, crime, child abuse, drug abuse, and the feelings of hopelessness in American society, and you can see that we live in the midst of intense spiritual warfare with the devil. But when all is said and done, I want to be standing on the side of victory. I may not be able to single-handedly change the world, but when my life ends I want to be able to declare: "I fought the good fight. I didn't grow weary and settle for less. I battled to the end."

How about you, young man? Are you up for the challenge?

Thankfully, winning the fight doesn't depend on our own strength, power, might, wisdom, or talent. God didn't call us to serve Him because we were the best, the biggest, or the baddest. He didn't call us for any reason except that He loves us, and by His power, He has an incredible destiny for each of our lives. But you will never fulfill your destiny until you believe it exists. You must believe that the God you serve is in absolute control and has a reason and plan for your life!

The Lord is the rock on which I stand. He is a fortress, a shelter, and the shield of my faith. It doesn't just say that in His Word, I know it from experience. He is the Truth by which I live. His dominion will never end. Don't you dare give up, young man. God has prepared a great victory for you if you're wise enough to claim it through "the good fight of faith."

Everything involving your destiny and character can only be won through faith. Everything you fight for must be obtained by faith. God's blessings, His healing, and forgiveness are all available. But you can only find them through faith. You say you need to grow in faith? Then dive into His Word. Aggressively hunger for its truth by reading it, studying it, and meditating on it.

If you will embrace the message and spirit of *Warriors,* you will create havoc for the devil. You have been called to be "revolutionies," men who will shine the light of God's Word into a sin-sick, dying generation. Will you be a brave man of courage? Do you have enough guts to stand and be identified with the cross of Jesus Christ?

Those who will answer the call and, as the Army might say, "Be all they can be," are my heroes. They aren't afraid to pay the price of sacrificing for the cause of Christ. When the world trains you to "Look out for number one" in everything you do, it seems scary to deny yourself and give Him your best. But this is essential for living a lifestyle of destiny and pleasing God.

At the beginning of Jesus's ministry, it was God's will that He go through a wilderness experience and into direct confrontation with Satan. If you want to know God's will and His destiny for your life, you must have the same tenacity to face the devil. You will face battles with him because he stands between you and God's best.

Will you join the fight to impact the world with the gospel of Jesus Christ? No matter who you are or where you live, you are called to make a great impact for God's glory. Student, businessman, lawyer, or tradesman, you all have a part to play. Seize your destiny. Implement the teachings of this book. It will bring a radical, spiritual dimension to your life like you could never imagine. Do it!

—*Phil Bonasso*
*Senior Director*
*Morning Star Ministries*
*Lomita, California*

# RESOURCES

The following is by no means a comprehensive list of men's ministries. They are ones that I have become familiar with over the years. Regardless of what church and ministries you link up with, be sure to find other men who can help disciple, strengthen, and encourage you in your Christian walk.

### Athletes International Ministry

A.I.M. is a collegiate and professional outreach ministry, forming missions teams, groups to do school assemblies, and men's discipleship groups. It also sponsors an annual international conference of Christian athletes. For more information, contact Larry Kerychuk, Executive Director, Athletes International Ministry, 100 W. Clarendon, Suite 910, Phoenix, AZ 85013, phone 602- 265-5959.

### Brotherhood Commission

A missions agency of the Southern Baptist Convention, the commission aims to involve men in spreading the gospel through missions projects, including disaster relief and volunteer construction. Its men's ministries department has produced Leading Men's Ministries, a how-to manual for starting men's ministries in a local church; and Legacy Builders Retreat Preparation Manual to help plan a men's retreat. The Brotherhood offers other male development studies and materials that are usable for men of all denominations. Contact Jim Burton, Director, Men's Ministries, Brotherhood Commission, 1548 Poplar Ave., Memphis, TN 38104. phone 901-272-2461, fax 901-726-5540.

## Champions for Christ

This ministry is dedicated to strengthening and equipping collegiate and professional athletes from across the nation. Says Darrell Green, defensive back for the Washington Redskins, "The ministry of Champions for Christ has played an important part in my spiritual development. It has been a pleasure to have CFC as a part of my life and team." Contact Greg Ball, Director, Champions for Christ, 4505 Spicewood Springs Rd., #307, Austin, TX 78759, phone 512-338-0433, fax 512-338-0451.

## Christian Men's Network

Best-selling author and lecturer Edwin Louis Cole spearheads this worldwide outreach to men. Declaring that Christlikeness and manhood are synonymous, Dr. Cole has been at the forefront of the men's movement. Pastors and church leaders worldwide use the CMN monthly video network, which specializes in equipping men to be Christ's disciples. For information about conferences, books, and audio and video teachings, write to the Christian Men's Network, P.O. Box 610588, Dallas, TX 75261, phone 817-283-2898, fax 817-685-9625.

## Christian Business Men's Committee of the USA

The CBMC seeks to impact the world by saturating the business and professional community with the gospel of Jesus Christ by establishing, equipping, and mobilizing teams that yield spiritual reproducers. Contact Christian Business Men's Committee, P. O. Box 3308, Chattanooga, TN 37404, phone 407-331-0095.

## Fellowship of Christian Athletes

Founded in 1954, FCA is the nation's oldest sports ministry. Its fellowship groups meet on high school and college campuses across the nation, and it holds summer sports camps where, over the years, thousands have accepted Christ. FCA also publishes a monthly magazine and a series of discipleship training materials. For more information, write to FCA at 8701 Leeds Rd., Kansas City, MO 64129, or call 816-921-0909, fax 816-921-8755.

### John Jacobs Evangelistic Association

A dynamic evangelistic outreaching featuring the "Power Team" and their incredible "feats of strength." The Power Team conducts citywide crusades targeting schools and families in the community. Their weekly "Power Connection" program is aired over the Trinity Broadcasting Network. For more information, contact the Power Team, P.O. Box 816404, Dallas, TX 75381-6404, phone 214-831-1990.

### Men's Leadership Ministries

The mission of Men's Leadership Ministries is to equip men in personal character and holiness, helping them lead the family, church, and nation. Bi-annual Men's National Congress. Contact Men's Leadership Ministries, P. O. Box 541104, Dallas, TX 75354, phone 214-239-9610.

### Professional Athletes Outreach

Based in the Seattle, Washington, area this outreach to professional athletes in major sports, including auto racing, is led by former pro football star Norm Evans. Its program includes continuing outreach to athletes and a series of national conferences on personal, family, and spiritual topics, held after the season concludes in each sport. For more information, contact Pro Athletes Outreach, P.O. Box 1044, Issaquah, WA 98027, phone 206-392-6300.

### Promise Keepers

This men's discipleship movement has swept the nation during the 1990s, attracting hundreds of thousands of men to its series of sold-out conferences in football stadiums and other arenas. The book, Seven Promises of a Promise Keeper, hit the best-seller list after its publication in 1994. It also offers a variety of resource materials and has various leadership conferences and men's meetings in dozens of cities. Contact Promise Keepers, P.O. Box 18376, Boulder, CO 80308, phone 303-421-2800, fax 303- 421-2918.

## Victory Campus Ministries International

This ministry strives to train Christians to impact the world with the gospel of Jesus Christ. It primarily focuses on university campuses around the world, establishing campus fellowships and discipling students to fulfill God's purposes for their lives. For further information about conferences, seminars, starting a campus group or the Victory School of Ministry, write to Tom Sirotnak, Victory Campus Ministries, P.O. Box 368, Harbor City, CA 90710.

## Vision America

Vision America's goal is to heal America's cities through small group fellowships of men. Directed at healing the lost art of self-esteem among men. Contact Vision America, 174 Wilshire Blvd., Casselberry, FL 32707, phone 407-331-0095.

# NOTES

## Introduction

1. "The Terrible Twenties," *Newsweek,* quoted in *13th Gen.: Abort, Retry, Ignore, Fail?* by Neil Howe and Bill Strauss (Vintage Books, 1993), 7.

## Chapter 1

1. *American Demographics* magazine, quoted in *13th Gen.: Abort, Retry, Ignore, Fail?* by Neil Howe and Bill Strauss (Vintage Books, 1993), 8.

2. Ann Landers, *Santa Cruz Sentinel* (October 25, 1984), B-5.

3. W.M. Hardenbrook, *Missing from Action* (Nashville: Thomas Nelson Publishers, 1987), 12.

4. Ibid., 17.

5. Quoted in *Commitment to Excellence* (Lombard, Ill.: Great Quotations, 1984), C-69.

6. I heard Kinchlow make this statement at a weekend conference sponsored by the Christian Men's Network. It also appeared in the introductory notes to *Maximized Manhood* by Edwin Louis Cole (Whittaker House, 1982).

## Chapter 2

1. Bobby Boyles, pastor of Eagle Heights Church in Oklahoma City, Okla. speaking at the 1994 annual meeting of the Southern Baptist Convention; quoted by *Baptist Press,* Nashville, Tenn; used with permission.

2. Bo Jackson and Dick Schapp, *Bo Knows Bo* (New York, N.Y.: Doubleday, 1990), 20.

3. I credit Ed Cole for this teaching. I heard it often and literally soaked it up into my spirit. It has been a key principle in my life and it can be in yours too.

## Chapter 3

1. This saying often appears as anonymous but is most often credited to Wesley. From *Illustrations Unlimited,* James Hewett, ed., © 1988, page 128; used by permission of Tyndale House Publishers, Inc.; all rights reserved.

2. Quoted in *The Mediator,* newsletter of Mastermedia International, vol. 9, no. 2.

3. *Illustrations Unlimited,* 254.

## Chapter 4

1. "The Young Fogies," *The Washington Post,* quoted in *13th Gen.: Abort, Retry, Ignore, Fail?* by Neil Howe and Bill Strauss (Vintage Books, 1993), 11.

2. I was first enlightened about this teaching when I read Ed Cole's book, *Maximized Manhood*.

3. D. James Kennedy, *Character and Destiny* (Zondervan Publishing House, 1994), 46.

4. Ibid., 46.

## Chapter 5

1. This saying often appears as anonymous but is most often credited to Wesley. From *Illustrations Unlimited*, James Hewett, ed., © 1988, page 305; used by permission of Tyndale House Publishers, Inc.; all rights reserved.

2. *Los Angeles Herald-Examiner* (May 5, 1987).

3. "Energized by Pulpit or Passion, the Public Is Calling, 'Gospel Grapevine' Displays Strength in Controversy over Military Gay Ban," *The Washington Post* (February 1, 1993).

4. John Bartlett, *Bartlett's Familiar Quotations*, 16th ed., Justin Kaplan, gen. ed., (Little, Brown and Company, 1992), 369.

## Chapter 6

1. According to the Patton Museum in Fort Knox, Kentucky, this is just one version of a series of speeches that Patton delivered between March and June of 1944 to newly-arriving units in England and Ireland.

2. *Illustrations Unlimited*, James Hewett, ed., © 1988, page 309; used by permission of Tyndale House Publishers, Inc.; all rights reserved.

3. Adapted from *Minister of Defense* by Reggie White with Terry Hill (Brentwood, Tenn.: Wolgemuth & Hyatt, 1991), 57–59; all rights reserved and used with permission of the author.

4. Quoted in the *Press-Telegram*, Long Beach, Calif., (February 8, 1994).

5. Edwin Louis Cole, *Real Man* (Thomas Nelson Publishers, 1992), 49, all rights reserved.

6. Ibid., 47.

7. R.C. Sproul, *Objections Answered*, reprinted in *Illustrations Unlimited*, James Hewett, ed., © 1988, 436; used by permission of Tyndale House Publishers, Inc.; all rights reserved.

## Chapter 8

1. *Illustrations Unlimited*, Hewett, ed., ©1988, 330; used by permission of Tyndale House Publishers, Inc.; all rights reserved.

2. Ibid., story told by Charles Krieg, 97.

3. Ibid., 336.

4. Ibid., statement by James Wharton, 335.

5. Ibid., 334.

6. Ibid., 194.

7. *The Book of Virtues*, compiled by William J. Bennett (Simon & Schuster, 1993), 186.

## Chapter 9

1. Quoted in *13th Gen.: Abort, Retry, Ignore, Fail?* by Neil Howe and Bill Strauss (Vintage Books, 1993), 147.
2. "Sex under Control" by Dr. Archibald Hart, *New Man* (November/December 1994), 36.
3. Quoted in Washington Watch, (Family Research Council, October 14, 1994), 1.
4. Quoted in "One Man Team," *Challenge* ( August 1994), 4.

## Chapter 10

1. *Illustrations Unlimited,* James Hewett, ed., © 1988, 56; used by permission of Tyndale House Publishers, Inc.; all rights reserved.

## Chapter 11

1. *Illustrations Unlimited,* James Hewett, ed., © 1988, 131; used by permission of Tyndale House Publishers, Inc.; all rights reserved.
2. Gordon Dalbey, *Healing The Masculine Soul* (Word Publishing, 1988), 122; used by permission.
3. Ibid., 122–123.

## Chapter 12

1. *13th Gen.: Abort, Retry, Ignore, Fail?* by Neil Howe and Bill Strauss (Vintage Books, 1993), 76.
2. Ibid., page 82.
3. Michael Oreskes, "U.S. Youth in the '90s: The Indifferent Generation," *Washington Post,* citing The *Times Mirror* Center for the People and Press Report and People for the American Way, *New York Times* (June 28, 1990), A-1.
4. Ibid.
5. *Time* (July 19, 1993), 30.
6. Matthew Henry and Thomas Scott, *Commentary on the Whole Bible,* (Thomas Nelson, 1979), 371.

## Chapter 13

1. *Illustrations Unlimited,* James Hewitt, ed., © 1988, 40; used by permission of Tyndale House Publishers, Inc.; all rights reserved.
2. Ibid., 40.
3. While I originally heard this story from my pastor, I later discovered it in *Illustrations Unlimited,* 160–161. It is credited to a man named James Aggrey.

## Chapter 14

1. *Illustrations Unlimited,* James Hewitt, ed., © 1988, 295; used by permission of Tyndale House Publishers, Inc.; all rights reserved.
2. Ibid., 128.
3. *Motivational Quotes,* (Lombard, Ill.,: Great Quotations, 1984), 76.
4. *The Book of Virtues,* compiled by William Bennett (Simon & Schuster, 1993), 541–542.

## Epilogue

1. John Bartlett, *Bartlett's Familiar Quotations,* 16th ed., Justin Kaplan, gen. ed., (Little, Brown and Company, 1992), 369.